WHAT EVERY PASTOR'S WIFE SHOULD KNOW

What every pastor's wife should know

RUTHE WHITE

TYNDALE HOUSE
Publishers, Inc.
Wheaton, Illinois

Third printing, August 1988
Library of Congress Catalog Card Number 85-51647
ISBN 0-8423-7932-0
Printed in the United States of America

Dedicated to my own TOs (theological offspring), Deanna and Jan, who grew up in the church parsonage and are now in partnership ministry with their husbands.

Deanna *is active in teaching, speaking, and choral work. She is married to Greg Bryant, who pastors a growing congregation in Southern California.*

Jan *is the wife of composer/producer/singer, Dan Burgess. She is a soloist and works with her husband in recording, and in Christian concerts throughout the nation.*

CONTENTS

■

PART
I

YOU
AND
YOUR
CALL

I was not called [to be a pastor's wife] by any group or agency. My call is from Jesus Christ himself, and from God the Father.

GALATIANS 1:2 (The Living Bible)

ONE

Who Is the Pastor's Wife, Anyway?

THE PASTOR'S WIFE IS THE ONLY WOMAN I KNOW WHO IS INTRODUCED BY HER HUSBAND'S PROFESSION: "THIS IS OUR PASTOR'S WIFE"!

According to Roy Coffman of *Partnership* magazine, a periodical geared to the needs of the pastor's wife, we are now over 400,000 strong. (That number does not include those outside the United States.)

My own research, from the returns of a blind sampling poll mailed to PWs (pastors' wives) across the nation, shows that we are talented, creative, conscientious, and caring individuals. Our duties are varied and our responsibilities demanding. We are, in most cases, overinvolved in the church ministry itself. One PW, in response to the questionnaire I mailed her, wrote:

> *I am the church secretary, office manager, bookkeeper, assistant music director, adult teacher, children's church*

coordinator, district representative of women's ministries, organist, member of a trio and of a choral group. I help supplement the family income by working part time as a school teacher. My husband and I have two children aged eleven and eighteen. Occasionally, I find myself resenting my role. The most difficult area of this ministry is in trying to help people, then having them cut my family to pieces through it all. I am happy in what I do, except that I would love to be able to stay at home to sew, draw, study, and decorate my house. My husband doesn't always have the time, or take time, to recognize my personal needs. (Sometimes he is understanding.) I live in a parsonage and this is often a problem for me. My schedule is so full there is no time to socialize with women other than those within our local congregation.

Is this beginning to sound familiar to you?

This letter is not that atypical. This PW may be a bit more involved than most, but the shocking news is: Most of the women who took time to answer my questionnaire agreed with this point of view. Many felt the demands upon both themselves and their husbands were too great. A large percentage of those living in parsonages are insecure about it and consider their housing to be an ongoing problem. Many would like more personal and individual identity within their roles and a better understanding from others toward their ministry.

I discovered that we, as pastors' wives, come from all backgrounds of life, having little or no training for our work. (A large percentage of women indicated they had no PW role model with whom they could identify.) We are often confused, frustrated about our roles, and can find almost no help in ascertaining what is expected of us. Material geared to our needs is often limited and we have to search to find what does exist. The same is not true of our preacher husbands. They are inundated with volumes of books to aid them in their ministry. Ongoing educational classes, seminars, conventions, and other programs provide them with ideas enabling them to be more effective in their work—while we wives are often left alone to grapple with many of the same problems they face!

It appears, from our lack of helpful resource material, that we are expected to have all the answers before knowing the questions. Because our roles are changing, and the guidelines nebulous, we cannot always determine what the priorities are; and that in itself is becoming a part of the problem! Some people assume that our growth as effective partners in ministry is, or should be, automatic. I wonder: *Do they think we are modified saints simply because we are married to pastors?* Do washing and ironing his clerical shirt, preparing his meals, and sleeping in the same bed with him make us spiritual? Can people possibly believe that we, through some form of religious osmosis, will become paragons of virtue? Are we any less human than they, those women who perform the same household tasks, but whose husbands work in other vocations?

The idea of such expectations sounds absurd! Yet it is highly possible that some of us went into our marriages with these same misconceptions. We may have unconsciously assumed that because our spouses were in theological training they would become akin to biblical apostles. It didn't take long after we said "I do" to discover that we, who are not so perfect ourselves, were married to men of like weaknesses. We found that our husbands were men, strongly motivated, and as anxious to succeed in their vocations as were men in all other professions. Because of this, and due to a growing understanding of the ministry, we have had to rethink our own identity at times. Some of us may even see our personal image as tied so closely to that of our husbands' that we cannot differentiate between his work, our self-image, and God's work.

As a result of this attitude, the PW may face such personality confusion that she can easily become a silent partner in her marriage and her relationship to the church. Then, if calamity, illness, or some other loss forces her husband to enter another vocation, the PW is left feeling she is a misfit in society. If her husband should die it is even worse. Her name is dropped, in most cases, from denominational mailing lists. She is no longer informed of ministers' wives' meetings, since her minister husband is no longer living. Often her insurance coverage is contingent upon her husband's ministerial status, and she is left out in the cold upon his death.

A vivacious young woman attended one of my seminar retreat sessions. I noticed her as she sat crying through the first two classes. When it was possible for me to get some time alone with her, I learned why she was weeping. She said:

> *My husband died from cancer less than two years ago. I was left with four children—two in college, a teenage son, and a girl under six. Although I did have to go to work to support myself and the children, that was not my greatest area of difficulty. My problem has been in finding myself outside of society, not fitting into the social realm at work or church. I am no longer a pastor's wife with the loving presence of people around me. Let's face it, I'm a misfit! If people could only understand how lonely I feel. It would help me so much if I were informed as to what was happening on a ministerial level and could still be considered worthy of some input from those with whom we have labored.*

There are other PWs who have husbands that may feel this way about their wives—that they are a nonentity; they don't count! And when we get down on ourselves during brief moments of our lives, it is common to feel that parishioners see us as little more than the "ruffled frill" of our husband's pastoral assignment. This attitude was clearly implied by the many PWs who indicated they did not like to be introduced as simply: "This is our pastor's wife." How many times have we heard a woman presented as: "My plumber's wife"? Those same women felt they wanted to be known as individuals rather than as the "bonus pack" to their husband's ministerial call.

The interesting factor is: Not one woman in the poll said she would change her position, even if she could. While we PWs may not like all of the conditions which surround our work, we do enjoy the privilege of shaping lives, being a co-laborer in the kingdom of God, and knowing we are a part of our husband's ministry. We realize that we are not that different from other women who sit in the church pew. We perform many of the same duties as they: We drive our sons to Little League, take our daughters to Girl Scouts, live on budgets, grocery shop, clean our floors, and do all the ordinary things of life. Only we do all these things in relation to our other role: being a pastor's wife!

Our problems often surface when we try to determine who we are, as individuals, within our role. You may be struggling with that difficulty.

Who Are *You* in Relation to Your Role?

You are an individual with unique personal talents and abilities. Your strengths and weaknesses, along with your other traits, are the qualities that distinguish you from any other pastor's wife. There never has been, nor ever will be, another person just like you. That is exactly the way God has planned his kingdom's growth. If you and your spouse have truly been called of God to minister in a specific area, then the Lord has given or will give you the resources needed for the work. God never asks us to do something without giving us the equipment we need.

Moses, the patriarchal leader of Israel, had to learn this lesson. When the great "I AM" called him and asked Moses (who had once lived in Pharaoh's house) to bring God's people out of bondage, Moses winced and began giving excuses as to why he couldn't do the job. You remember— he reminded God about his stuttering, slow speech. The lame emotional crutch Moses used just didn't hold up with

God—he couldn't get by with it! Sometimes you and I act just like him. We get all "strung out" looking at what we think we don't have, forgetting what God has given us to work with. It takes the Apostle Paul to make us understand what our ability and strength can be. He says of himself and us:

> For I can do everything God asks me to with the help of Christ who gives me the strength and power (Phil. 4:13, TLB).

Once we get bogged down in our feelings of inadequacy we seem to react in one of two ways: 1) We begin to seek God for his strength and guidance; or, 2) we draw back for fear of failure, attempting only those things at which we feel highly confident. By failing to recognize God at work in us we never allow the heavenly Father to bring about growth in our lives. We instead spend our energies in a nonproductive manner.

It is highly important that you, as a minister's wife, always remember you are needed, that you have something to give, and learn to give it within the framework of your own personality. My father, a preacher himself, once said to me: "Sis, be what you are, nothing more and nothing less. If you try being someone you aren't, no one will be there; you won't, the person you are trying to imitate won't, and God's best will not be upon your life!"

You Are God's Personalized Gift to Your Husband

When I say you are God's special gift to the man with whom you live, and who is your pastor on Sunday, I am not telling you to sit on the front pew with a banner in your hand reminding him of it. No! Neither will you need to prod, force, cajole, or manipulate him into accepting you as such. If he has any spiritual insight he will understand that for himself. If, by chance, you are married to one of those men (there are some around) who simply does not have the ability to appreciate you in a Christ-loving way, likely as not, his ministry will be short-lived! On the other hand, if you feel loved and accepted by your spouse you can handle most any problem you face. What other people think becomes less important when you know you are accepted, loved, and appreciated by the man whose working clothes you press.

While you may not like all of the demands others lay upon you and the "glass house" in which you live, you will find your position much more tolerable when you fully comprehend your life as under God's directive. Knowing this will assist you toward a better understanding of your responsibilities. How you choose to carry out those duties becomes a personal matter between this triad: God, your spouse, and yourself. Whatever method the three of you use in accomplishing it is left to your options.

I am pleased that God has given us New Testament principles to replace Old Testament legalism. A law is unequivocally sure, a "thus saith"; whereas a principle is the grounds upon which we base our actions, the essential material that governs our motives. Under the law, a decision was made, a rule enforced. Under grace, a position is stated and we are told to "seek first the kingdom of God"; then we are left to give our personal allegiance freely.

We as individuals must make decisions based upon biblical soundness. But that does not mean we, as PWs, will all come out looking like mechanical saints. God didn't make us robots to be wound up, plugged in, and set in motion by a congregation of people. He gave us choices! While you may be pleased to know those choices, or options, are yours, you still cannot forget you are married to God's gift to the church.

Your Husband Is God's Gift to the Church
As a PW you will do well to consider these two alternatives in decision-making; 1) You can be your husband's greatest blessing; or, 2) you may become his worst hindrance. There seems

to be no middle road on the issue. You cannot disassociate yourself from this fact any more than you can walk away from your responsibility toward God. You are a vital part of the kingdom of God. The Apostle Paul in speaking to the church at Ephesus reminds us of the importance of our husband's work and ours. He writes:

> . . . *and he gave some, apostles; and some, prophets; and some, evangelists; and some, pastors and teachers (Eph. 4:11, KJV).*

The emphasis, at this point, should be on the words, *"he gave."* To the world, *he gave* his Son; to the church *he gave* pastors and teachers; to your husband, *he gave* you! My PW friend Betty Willis says: "Woman was God's idea *after all!*"

Since your husband is God's gift to the church, for the purpose of edifying the saints and equipping them for work in the kingdom, and you are God's gift to him—shouldn't you be willing to accept the importance of that call?

YOU Are a Woman in a Key Position in the Church

As a woman in a key position in the church you dare not minimize your role. Like it or not, what you are and the manner in which you conduct yourself will reflect upon your husband. You are an extension of what his ministry represents. Many times those with whom you are in contact will judge your husband's character and ministry by your reputation. I know of no other profession which places spouses under a greater load, in respect to actions, than does the ministry. At the same time, I can think of nothing greater than having the privilege of working with people and watching them grow into mature, vital, and productive Christians.

GROWTH PLAN

Ask yourself:
1. What do I want to do with my life? (Answer in twenty-five words or less.)
2. Am I willing to accept personal responsibility for what I am?
3. Am I ready for God to use me where he sees best?
4. Can I recognize God at work in me right now, right where I am?
5. How does Romans 8:28 apply to my present situation?

". . . and we know that all that happens to us is working for our good if we love God and are fitting into his plans" (TLB).

Suggested Reading:
LaHaye, Tim and Phillips, Bob, *Anger Is a Choice,* Zondervan
Packer, J. I., *Knowing God,* InterVarsity Press

For who makes you different from anyone else?
What do you have that you did not receive? And if you
did receive it, why do you boast as though you did not?
1 CORINTHIANS 4:7 (NIV)

TWO

How Does the Pastor's Wife Differ . . . or Does She?

THE PASTOR'S WIFE IS THE

ONLY WOMAN I KNOW

WHO IS ASKED TO WORK

FULL TIME WITHOUT

PAY ON HER HUSBAND'S

JOB, IN A ROLE NO ONE

HAS YET DEFINED.

Gina, a charming young pastor's wife, was sitting beside me in the restaurant where we were eating lunch. A beam of sunlight was coming through the window and dancing across the ends of Gina's freshly permed, reddish-brown hair. I had only to look at her, a picture of natural beauty, tall and thin with great bone structure, to understand why she had been successful as a part-time model.

"Once a model, but no more!" she said to me. "My minister husband and I have been married for eight years now. My work has changed considerably since meeting him. Right now, if you were to ask me what I am doing I would have to tell you I am tired, frustrated, and don't understand either who I am as a person, or just what my role is as a pastor's wife."

Her frustrations were not that unusual. I had already interviewed a number of PWs and knew that many were hurting. What concerned me most about my young friend Gina was the tired expression on her face, and what I was hearing through her voice as she spoke with me. As I listened further I was soon to understand the reason for her fatigue.

We came to this city two years ago for the purpose of pioneering a new church. After renting a house in which to live we began having Bible studies and prayer meetings in our living room. Our newly acquired congregation soon outgrew our home. That growth forced us into making some decisions we had not anticipated, at least not so quickly. It was then that I became keenly aware of the hard facts of our work—I knew I was the preacher's wife!

Since there was not enough money to rent both a house and a place for worship, my husband and I discussed the matter. Within a few days we found ourselves packing the furniture from our three-bedroom house, placing it in storage, and moving into a twenty-two-foot motor home. The three of us, my husband, myself, and our then one-year-old son, Josh, lived in those cramped facilities for two years. During the time we lived there I was working in the local bank to supplement our small income. (Even though our congregation has now grown, I still work part time.)

Just one month ago we moved out of the R.V. unit back into a rented house. What a treat it was taking all my personal belongings out of storage. After not being able to use them for two years I felt like a new bride with each box I opened.

Apologizing for having shared her feelings with me, expressing guilt for not understanding her own emotions, Gina talked on:

> There has been no one to help me! You see, I was not reared in a minister's home, as was my husband. In fact, I had been a Christian only a short time when I met Gary. So, you can see that what I have learned in this role as a pastor's wife has been on my own through trial and error.
>
> I love the church work and want to carry my part of the responsibility. I am very much a part of our church program. There is a sense in which my work at the church is gratifying. I am active in teaching our Children's Forum on Sunday morning, instruct a Temple Toners class one night a week, and assist in the music department of the church. All of these things are a challenge to me! On the other hand, I sometimes find myself feeling that I am being used. To be honest, I feel depleted, emotionally drained, and spiritually discouraged.

Depleted, drained, discouraged! Those were words I was hearing more and more frequently from PWs of all age groups and denominational backgrounds. I knew many of us had been where Gina was. I could remember times when I had struggled with the same issues of financial, emotional, and physical stress. Naturally, my first human impulse, as I sat there thinking over my own past twenty-five-years-plus in the ministry, was to "turn spiritual." I wanted to tell Gina how wonderful it was to trust in God through the moments of trial, tell her about his faithfulness in meeting my family's needs, and about all the wonderful answers to prayer. While all those things would have been true, I knew in my own heart that Gina loved the Lord as much as I did, and this was not the time for testimonials.

Her problems were real and she needed to talk about them. Above all, she did not need me to pat her on the head and tell her, "Honey, you just pray about them and they will go away." She was reaching out to me, wanting me to listen without judging her motives, to understand her emotions without placing more guilt upon her. I was also reminded that this generation of PWs is faced with a different set of problems than those known by women in ministry of any other era.

You are given options, choices, and asked to make decisions that are unique to your culture. Never in the known history of the church world has there been a busier time than today. The local body of corporate believers is organized to the hilt—each age grouping within the church having its own programs skillfully managed, activities often overlapping—with the pastor being expected to attend them all. (One PW told me she was required to attend three church functions in one evening. This meant she had to go from one meeting to another within a span of a few hours.) Historically, this was not a part of the early church structure. And look at the founding fathers in the 1800s and 1900s. They often served more than one parish, traveling on horseback or in a buggy for hours. This made it virtually impossible for their wives to accompany them on the circuit.

You are expected to go . . . go . . . go! Above all else, you must be highly visible. Poor Suzanna Wesley, with all her kids, would never have had a chance as a twentieth-century PW. She spent too much time in the rearing of her children to have been accepted by most boards in today's churches.

You differ from the average woman in another way: As a PW you are subject to the whims of the people who hire your husband. There is a sense of insecurity that comes in knowing that you are accountable to those persons who are responsible for either hiring or firing your mate. Women whose husbands work on secular jobs are relatively free from this kind of pressure. Whatever may occur on their spouse's job is usually settled in a professional manner, strictly between the employer and him. The wife, in most cases, does not enter into it.

You are unlike other women because you are given little or no room for human error. If you happen to "goof," your husband pays the penalty for it. This, in turn, puts a great deal of stress upon the clergy marriage. Both partners, you and your husband, are constantly having to walk a psychological tightrope. I know, because I have lived it. There was one time in particular when a misunderstanding developed in our church over something I did.

Being the teacher of a large young adult Sunday school class in our church, I planned a weekend retreat for those in attendance. It was the policy that all church-sponsored activity be posted on the office master calendar. The committee working with me went through the proper channel of clearing the dates and posting them. One week before our planned retreat, we discovered that an independent group of recreational vehicle owners within our congregation had arbitrarily planned a camping trip for the same weekend. They had not placed their activity on the calendar because, according to them, "This is not a church-sponsored event."

Having both groups away on the same Sunday meant we would be taking out most of the choir members, the pianist, and many of the teachers from the morning worship services. (We had two services in order to accommodate the crowds in attendance.) Knowing I could not cancel my reservation without paying the camp a specified amount, I asked to meet with some of the members from the other group. It was my hope that, since there were no monies involved, they would agree to rearrange their trip. Well, the matter got blown clear out of perspective! It looked, for a while at least, as though the whole church would be in a "ruckus" over it. I wondered if my husband's position would be threatened. Not many women with husbands in secular jobs would face that kind of insecurity over such a trivial matter.

One of the most obvious ways in which you differ from other women is that you are not totally free to do your own thing or to go your own way. There are some things you dare not do, not just for your sake, but for the cause of God's kingdom. A situation or action may not be wrong in itself; but it is simply not best for the given Cause. Again, Paul tells us that all things may be lawful, but not all things are expedient. *The Living Bible* puts this verse in readable twentieth-century language:

> *I can do anything I want to if Christ has not said no, but some of these things aren't good for me. Even if I am allowed to do them, I'll refuse to if I think they might get such a grip on me . . . (1 Cor. 6:12).*

Another noticeable way in which you differ from other women is in your role. I mentioned in an earlier chapter that our roles have never been defined. That could be either good or bad! If you were to ask another PW what you are supposed to be doing, she would give you the answer as it relates to her. But if you were to ask that same question of another, the answer would be altogether different. Each person would reply according to her own frame of reference. Since no one can give you clear-cut guidelines, you are left with the responsibility of establishing your own working guidelines.

You differ because you have an undefined role, and therefore that role is always changing. The expectation level varies within each congregation of people. Some churches feel they are hiring two persons for the price of one, while others want the wife to have no part in her husband's ministry. When you, as a PW, have to move between these two extremes, you may feel as if you are caught in a gravitational tug-of-war. I found myself in that situation once and it threw me off guard.

My husband accepted a transfer from a small community

setting where I was active in a teaching ministry. The city itself provided little or no recreational facilities for its youth. Having teenaged daughters of my own, I worked hard at organizing youth functions that centered around our church social hall. When we left there and moved to another parish, I was soon to discover a different philosophy. The board of directors of the new church would not permit me to teach on the Sunday school staff. The reason they gave was: "We are afraid if you teach, as the pastor's wife, it will disrupt some of the other existing classes. People might want to go to your sessions instead of attending ours."

Needless to say, I was chafing, knowing there was a definite need, having the burden to work in that area, but not being permitted to do so. Finally, after one year, I was allowed to contact anyone who was not already attending our Sunday school. If some would agree to come, I could teach them. It was made perfectly clear to me that no adult already in attendance would be given permission to transfer into my class. The arrangement was acceptable to me. All I asked for was the opportunity to teach. However, I had quite an adjustment coming from one congregation where I was so highly visible, and the church was paying a house-keeper so I could devote myself to the work, then finding myself in such a "touchy" situation. I wondered, *had I been wrong in my previous involvement? What did the church really want from me, and what was God teaching me through it all?*

I wish I could tell you I handled those feelings in a saintly manner. Not at all! There were brief moments in which I resented my husband for having placed me in such a precarious position. My pride and ego were affected by my feelings of personal rejection. Still, I knew I could not blame Claude for having come to the church. He had never accepted a pastorate without our being in total agreement on the matter. It was just that I couldn't put the pieces together because my role had changed so drastically. I wasn't mad at God;

he was not the problem! I was angry with short-sighted people who would not permit me to work in the area of "my calling." The expectation level of the people was so different from that which I had been conditioned to accept, I soon found myself having to redirect my thinking. Believe me, that took time, energy, and lots of prayer!

Another PW wrote me just a few weeks ago about how she was struggling with many of these same problems.

> *For the first time in twenty-five years of church work I am beginning to feel that I am not needed. I don't know what the people expect of me. There is no place for me to work within the church structure. What do I do, go out and get a job, or what? I have never worked outside the church, but I must find an outlet for my abilities.*

You may not have this problem . . . not yet! Rest assured that in the natural course of your life there will be moments when you will feel discouraged, as though you have lost your moorings and need some guidance. What really concerns me is not that you have these moments, because we all do; but when those feelings overwhelm you, to whom can you go? The PW cannot turn to another woman in the church. The one who wrote the above letter stated that she didn't know if her husband understood her needs or not. If you aren't sure you can talk with your mate, and if you are locked into a church situation in a small community, where do you go?

Many PWs are finding their strongest support among other ministers' wives. Even then, there is a tendency to hold back, and we, as PWs, often do little to help each other. We overlook others' needs, leaving them alone within the walls of their denominational setting, while we go our own ways. There has been almost no unified effort among us for the passing down of information, developing skills, building resource material, or mutual sharing. We may be guilty of having neglected the words of Paul to Timothy (2 Tim. 2:1, 2) when he encouraged him, saying:

Oh, Timothy, my son, be strong with the strength Christ Jesus gives you. For you must teach others those things you and many others have heard me speak about. Teach these truths to trustworthy men [women] who will, in turn, pass them on to others (TLB).

No one can rightfully accuse us of being selfish by nature. There is, perhaps, no group that is more unselfish in motive, loving in disposition, and caring as are we PWs. But even with all these wonderful qualities it is highly possible we are oblivious to the needs of the younger minister's wife and/or the woman in partnership ministry who lives across town. We are often kept too busy fighting our own battles, taking care of our own families. We are so wrapped up in our secure denominational blankets, we forget the coldness that the new pastor's wife (who has just moved into town), may be feeling. I pause to ask myself, and you, are we faithfully carrying out the command of God in Galatians 6:10 to be especially kind to those who are of the household of faith?

You may be wondering what all of this has to do with you personally. First, you are not an island unto yourself. Second, you do have a far-reaching responsibility, one that crosses all barriers. Third, at some time you too may need the help of another. Fourth, as a PW, no one can understand your needs as well as the person who has been where you are.

1. Ask God to give you a sincere appreciation for what he is doing through other people's ministries, as well as in your own.
2. Remember that while you may be grappling with your own problems of rejection, identity, and/or the need for acceptance, you are not unique in those struggles. (Even if you have your life under positive control, that is all the more reason for you to reach out to someone else!)

3. Understand that being a PW presents challenges that make you highly vulnerable. You are different! You maintain a life-style that can only be understood by those who also work in ministry. For that reason you need others. Your spiritual-emotional self demands that you have times of laughing with others, crying on another's shoulder, and knowing someone else understands! For it is by this example that others will know you really are his disciple.

GROWTH PLAN

List the names of ten pastors' wives who live within five miles of you.

PHONE

1. _____ _____
2. _____ _____
3. _____ _____
4. _____ _____
5. _____ _____
6. _____ _____
7. _____ _____
8. _____ _____
9. _____ _____
10. _____ _____

Take this list with you when you have your devotions and ask God to give you a personal concern for their needs. Mention their names individually in prayer.

If there is one from whom you feel estranged, ask yourself "Why?" and make her a special object of your prayers for one week.

Suggested Reading:
Briscoe, Jill, *Thank You for Being a Friend*, Zondervan

We do not dare to classify or compare ourselves with some who commend themselves. When they measure themselves by themselves and compare themselves with themselves, they are not wise. We, however, will not boast beyond proper limits, but will confine our boasting to the field God has assigned to us, a field that reaches even to you.

2 CORINTHIANS 10:12, 13 (NIV)

THREE

Who Are the Image Makers?

THE PASTOR'S WIFE CAN

HAVE JUST ABOUT ANY-

THING SHE WANTS, SO

LONG AS SOMEONE GIVES

IT TO HER, SHE CAN

MAKE IT HERSELF, OR SHE

CAN BUY IT FOR HALF

PRICE; EVEN THEN, SHE

MAY FEEL COMPELLED

TO EXPLAIN WHERE SHE

GOT IT.

Eddie Fisher, the singer, talked about the image makers of his profession in his book, *Eddie*.[1] He told of an incident when he was handed a black tuxedo and a black turtleneck

[1] Eddie Fisher, *Eddie: My Life, My Loves,* Harper & Row

sweater and asked to wear them for his next performance. On his neck was to be worn a pendant made up of a forty-carat blue sapphire stone, surrounded by square-cut baguette diamonds. The singer said he didn't want to wear the gaudy jewelry and black tux, but it was all a part of the image he was being asked to project.

We probably have read about the stars, starlets, and other Hollywood types, thinking to ourselves, "What a sham!" Yet many of us never stop to consider that hype is found not only in Tinsel Town. Every organized group within our society tends to project its own image. People associated with a group often emulate their leader in mannerisms, modes of behavior, and codes of dress; the leader, in turn, becomes the image maker.

People in the church, and even PWs, are no less prone to these temptations. We have our own theological phrases that help us protect our images—and we know how to use them! We know that if we say the right words enough times in one conversation, we will sound really spiritual. We become masters of our trade, donning wifely uniforms and dancing to the cadence of the image makers. Our actions are often motivated by a strong desire to please, to do those things that are expected of us. Sometimes we don't even know what people are wanting us to do and be.

I wonder: Should we hang six-inch crosses around our necks, wear "Jesus Loves You" buttons on our dress lapels, and plaster our cars with bumper stickers? Is that what the image makers think we ought to be? Or are we expected to be something of a mixture between a living saint and an unseen angel?

I once asked a group of ladies at a retreat where I was speaking (not PWs), what they thought was the pastor's wife image. The number one thing they said was that she had to be musical. That was almost considered the criterion for acceptance. Each lady commented about her ideal pastor's wife—how she should look, comb her hair, and wear her clothes. They insisted she needed a "preacher's wife" look.

What is that look?

Most of us agree, we dare not be too well dressed or it will appear that we are a "clothes horse." If we have a flair for putting our wardrobe together we are branded as proud and haughty. Even if something nice is given to us, we often feel it best not to wear it. We are afraid it will be a little better, perhaps, than Sister DoMore's. Or, we may be afraid our husband's position will be threatened by a too-sharp image of the pastor's wife.

We women have to work through this much more than do our husbands. The church does not hold them in the same kind of straightjacket mold. They like him to have that well-starched look. The businessmen of the congregation want him to maintain his image in the community. We, on the other hand, are permitted to have most anything we want, so long as someone gives it to us, we make it ourselves, or we find it on sale. The congregations holding us captive to this archaic standard derived from the church's dark ages.

Do you remember when Ruth Graham, wife of evangelist Billy Graham, was given a fur coat? Every PW knew the reason Ruth gave that coat away. Besides being a conscientious and caring woman, Ruth Graham knew that it would not be best for her to wear the fur coat, at least not at that time. (I hope someone has given her another one and she can enjoy it.) I really do admire her for what she was willing to do for the sake of God's work. There are times in each of our lives when it becomes necessary to make concessions to the moment. However, I am not sure I could have been as unselfish in nature as was Mrs. Graham. I think I might have been tempted to keep the coat. Up to this point, I have not had to face a similar decision. I have had other temptations to deal with, though. Such as the day I wore my fur-trimmed coat to church for the first time and overheard a parishioner saying, "I bet she spends all her husband's salary on clothes."

After hearing that statement I felt, as most PWs are inclined to, that I had to explain. So, very much to my husband's displeasure, because he felt it to be a personal matter, I went to the man, giving him a rundown on the cost. "My fur collar was picked up at a garage sale for five dollars; the fabric from which I made my coat is upholstery material; the total cost was about twenty dollars," I told him. Today the man who made that comment is one of our dearest and closest friends. He often chuckles about what he said and continues to tease me about it. The truth was that when I traipsed into the sanctuary wearing the coat I had moved away from the trap of the image makers.

Image makers are found in every congregation. They often expect us to run our families, participate in church activities, and do everything according to their preconceived ideas. Many times a task is expected to be done exactly as Sister So-and-So did it (in most cases she is the former pastor's wife). One lady told how she handled such a situation:

> *We had just accepted a new pastorate. The ladies in our church group were sitting around the table working on a project together. One of the women began talking about how much I differed from their former pastor's wife. I felt a little bit of a "dig" because I could not do some things the other woman had done. While I had never met her, they made me feel she must have been an angel. Soon the conversation turned and the women seated with me began talking about how much they loved my husband's ministry. As lovingly and kindly as I knew how, I turned to the women and asked, "Do you think God has called my husband to be your pastor?"*
>
> *"Yes," they replied.*
>
> *"Then surely you don't think for a moment that God*

wants my husband living with the other pastor's wife!"
The women laughed and that solved my problem.

I can't say that method is to be recommended. Obviously, it worked in this woman's case. But we all know that living in another woman's shadow can be a parsonage nightmare. This is especially true if you are a young, inexperienced PW. If, by chance, you follow another PW who was a whiz bang at organization, had endless energy and lots of ability, you probably will be expected to equal what she did. On the other hand, if the woman living in the manse before you was somewhat less desirable in her mannerisms, you will be penalized for her negative influence. You may be held in abeyance for a while until you are accepted on your own merits. There are some ways in which you can learn to deal with this problem objectively.

Take People Off the Defensive

You can take people off the defensive by reversing the roles. While the "braggart" stands at the threshold of your emotions, describing the wonderful person whose image you are expected to live up to—agree with him. Pick up on the conversation by referring to that woman in a caring and loving way. Jesus taught his disciples the principle of making friends quickly with their opponents (Matt. 5:25). If you learn to do this, you will be giving yourself the opportunity to rethink and regroup. You will also show that you can deal with the successes of others without feelings of jealousy. As amazing as it may seem, there are persons who take pleasure in "testing" the new pastor's wife. They may even look for some visible negative reaction from you that will give them clues to your personality. If you remain positive in your attitude, seldom will people pursue a subject they feel you are unresponsive toward.

**Try to Understand
Where the Other Person Is Coming From**

In seeking to better understand where people are coming from, you will discover they have a *frame of reference*. Also, you will find there are basically two kinds of people who are prone to think of what *was* as better than what *is*. They are: 1) The group who delights in "sizing" you up. Those persons come to you acting as though they were the most ardent supporters of the former pastor—when in reality that is not true. We should be careful before making quick judgments. Time is always our best measuring tool. 2) There are also people who have a deep and lasting respect for their former leadership. Try not to forget, in most instances, that the former pastor's wife stood by them during a time of crisis. Losing a person who has given emotional and spiritual support can be traumatic. Those who were helped by the former pastor and his wife may look at you wondering how you are going to respond to their needs. They are struggling, just as you are, so permit them to have a short grieving period. In most cases, in time, they will build a loving relationship with you. There is no occasion when your leadership qualities are made more visible than when you give others permission to love, without questioning their motives, allowing them to love freely (even if it's directed toward the other pastor's wife).

Don't Perpetuate the Wrong Image

There is a sense in which we tend to perpetuate the image the congregation has of us. We try to live on the pedestal they have created, and that is a big mistake. We are not built to stand on marble columns, in a motionless religious pose. God has ordained us, first, as Christians, to touch base with life, allowing Christ to supply the day-to-day needs of our lives. In order to do this you and I will have to become vulnerable. Sometimes parishioners are shocked by this!

One day I was cleaning my kitchen floor when the doorbell rang. My hair was pulled back from my face and I had on my old grubbies, hoping to finish the day's cleaning before dressing to go out for the evening. When I stepped up to the door and opened it, one of the young women from my Bible class was standing there. Her first reaction upon seeing me was: "Thank God, you *are* human! I have never seen you before without that preacher's wife look. Now I know you are not unlike me."

The spiritual "pedestal syndrome" can become a psychological crutch—something akin to a prop! I have observed PWs who seem so spiritual, one would think they lived with their heads in the stars. They never seem to have a problem; their husbands are perfect; if they have kids, they would make you believe they are angels; even their dogs bark, "Praise the Lord!" At least to hear the women tell it! All of this is part of the image they are protecting.

Remember that there were image makers in the early church too. In Jesus' day they followed him, dogging his footsteps, hoping to become a part of the kingdom they imagined he was about to set up. "Turn our stones into bread, overthrow our oppression and set us up an earthly kingdom," they begged of him.

Judas sprang from among that same group of image makers. He tried to force Jesus into becoming what he was not. Our Lord was confident in understanding his messiahship. Some theologians feel that the betrayal kiss Judas placed upon Christ was an action stemming from Judas' zeal toward the kingdom. He wanted the Roman yoke, which bound the Jewish people, to be broken. Perhaps that was not an ignoble wish . . . it was simply a misguided image of what he expected from the Messiah. Yet the Lord was not deterred from his primary purpose of reaching the cross to die for all mankind. The cross became his objective; people, circumstances—nothing would prevent him from doing that. Luke, the apostle, tells us, ". . . he stedfastly set his face to go to Jerusalem" (Luke 9:51, KJV). We are in big trouble when we feel the image others might have of us is more important than Christ's image in us. Josh McDowell deals with this subject most effectively throughout his book, *His Image, My Image.*[2]

Our Own Image May Be Distorted

What we think people want us to be could be nothing more than a distorted image of what we would like to be. Because of this, we may place demands upon ourselves that are totally unreasonable. Before getting too involved in what this means, let us consider the following questions:

1. *Does "the need" always mean we have to do something?* One pastor's wife sat tearfully pouring her heart out to me, saying, "We have a small church. I have two children under the age of five. On Sundays I feed and dress my family, drive our Sunday school bus to pick up other children, teach a class, play the piano for worship, teach children's church, and then deliver the kids home on the bus." Do you wonder that that woman was having some emotional problems?
2. *Does the burden always constitute the "call"?* Jesus didn't think so, because he told the disciples to ". . . pray to the one in charge of the harvesting, and ask him to recruit more workers for his harvest fields" (Matt. 9:38, TLB).
3. *Is it possible for us to organize areas of church ministry more quickly than we can train workers to fill the positions?* So long as we have churches there will be new demands. There are always those persons who have need of more. If Jesus were pastoring in this twentieth century he would overturn more than the money changers. I wonder how he would respond to the demand for more activities. We all hear the clamor of our society asking for more and more social involvement, as they beg us

[2]Josh McDowell, *His Image, My Image*, Here's Life

44

to turn their "stones into bread." *Get us money, money, money!*

Not one PW is totally free from these pressures. We have to live with them, adjust our lives around them. While there is no possible way to walk away from the image makers, we can build on the ministry God has given us. Still, somewhere along the way, we must learn to say, "No!"

GROWTH PLAN

1. How much pressure do I permit others to place upon me to fulfill a PW image?
2. Does the pressure come from one or two persons within the church structure?
3. Do I play a part or perpetuate an image in which I am highly uncomfortable?
4. Can I recognize the difference between what others demand and what God expects?
5. What are my alternatives in dealing with the image makers?

Suggested Reading:
Demaray, Donald E., *Watch Out for Burnout: Its Signs, Prevention, and Cure,* Baker
Greenfield, Guy, *We Need Each Other,* Baker
Minirth, Frank, and Meier, Paul, *Happiness Is a Choice: Overcoming Depression,* Baker
Peale, Norman Vincent, *Have a Great Day,* Revell

So then every one of us shall give account of himself [herself] to God.
ROMANS 14:12 (KJV)

FOUR

Building Your Own Self-image

IF YOU DO NOT KNOW

WHO YOU ARE AS A

PERSON YOU WILL NEVER

KNOW WHO YOU ARE

AS A PASTOR'S WIFE.

You need to discover who you are as a person before you will ever find fulfillment as a minister's wife. There will be a thousand voices crying out to tell you who you are and what you are supposed to be doing. Worse still, you will be tempted to listen as you are being pulled by each one, in all directions, becoming psychologically fragmented and soon "burned out."

Those same voices will impose guilt and place demands upon you that are too heavy for you to carry. Then your responsibilities, both real and imagined, will "gnaw" at your insides until you are unable to carry out the simplest duties of your household. One PW wrote me about what was happening to her in this respect. She said:

Dear Mrs. White,

I don't feel worthy to answer your questionnaire. I'm too discouraged and weary to give honest answers. I love the Lord, but am so tired of the ministry (thirty-four years).

Sincerely,
Pat

You can rest assured *someone* has placed guilt and demands upon Pat that helped to bring her to this point of desperation. And it wasn't God! The interesting note is not that she was weary and discouraged, but that she felt unworthy. Did she have those feelings of unworthiness because she was tired and discouraged? If that were true, we would all get knocked out of the Christian work force at some time during our lives.

Unfortunately, we as PWs have come to believe that it is quite all right for everyone else to become weary and take a leave of absence from their work. Sunday school teachers, choir members, women's directors, and anyone else involved in church ministry can take time off—*but we can't!* We have been conditioned to feel we are less than spiritual if we allow ourselves to get run down physically or *emotionally.* I stress the word "emotions" because the ministry runs the gamut of our emotional self. One minute we are holding a newborn in our arms, rejoicing with the proud parents. A half hour later we may be across town, weeping with another set of parents whose only child was killed in an automobile accident. Our feelings go up and down like an escalator as we learn to weep with those who weep, and to laugh with those who know laughter. The great tragedy of our work is that too few of us have learned the right balance between tears and laughter. We have never learned how to relax or to maintain a good emotional balance.

If we have a poor self-image we often berate ourselves, knowing that, after we have done all we could, there are needs yet unmet. We are also reminded, by experience, that tomorrow could very well be a repetition of the same roller-coaster emotional involvement we are having today. Howard Hendricks, the well-known Sunday school authority, is said to have been paid to evaluate the working schedule of a young minister. After following the man around for a few days, Howard told him, "I know what your problem is. You are not giving yourself enough 'think time.' " We PWs often become so involved with the other person's need, we forget that we too are human. We don't give ourselves the same opportunity for feeling, for letting our emotions wind down, as we permit other people.

One of our problems is in seeing other PWs who seem to have their lives put together, while our lives are being fragmented and torn. We don't understand why they are never pushed or driven by the compulsion we feel. Upon observing how other women are handling their responsibilities, we compare ourselves and feel we fall short. Our self-concept is reduced to zero and we feel we are a failure.

When your self-image is low it becomes increasingly difficult to differentiate between your *worth* before God and your *worthlessness*. To understand the difference is the first step in the development of a good self-image. You are *worth* God sending his Son to die for you.

I like the manner in which Dr. Richard Dobbins, of Emerge Ministries in Munroe Falls, Ohio, deals with this topic in his series, *The Believer and His Mental Health*.[3]

> *Your self-concept consists of what you believe about yourself. The reason your self-concept is so important is that everything you look at in life is viewed through the self-image. None of us lives simply with the fact of life, we live with the story we tell ourselves about the fact of our lives.*

Dr. Dobbins, in his series, provides us with a method of developing a good self-image from a poor one. He says

[3]Leader's Guide, *The Believer and His Mental Health*, Richard Dobbins, Totally Alive Publications

we must know that we are lovable, valuable, forgivable, and changeable! He gives a touching insight into his own childhood problem of knowing his mother had died at his birth. He once told a group of leaders how he had grown up with a kind of guilt feeling, thinking himself responsible for his own mother's death. He said:

> As I grew older I would go to my mother's grave and weep, knowing she had died to give me life. Soon after accepting Christ as my personal Savior, I went back to the cemetery, stood at the simple marker over Mother's body, and marveled at the Grace of God . . . how He loved me . . . by allowing me to live . . . even after Mother's death.

What had changed? Nothing, except his own self-image! Is it any wonder Richard Dobbins talks about the keys that unlock our self-concepts as being found in knowing we are *lovable, valuable, forgivable,* and *changeable?*

What powerful words these are! Before you read any further, why don't you stop right now and repeat them to yourself. Let your ears hear what your mouth is saying. Say these four words until your heart can join in on the chorus: loved, valued, forgiven, and changed!

One sure way in which you can bolster your ailing ego is finding your own niche. You can begin now to work toward discovering your place in the ministry by accepting yourself as an authentic person.

Finding Your Own Niche

Once you have reached the place in your life that you are not afraid to be your own person, you will also be free to pursue your own "call." Don't tell me you have no talent, because you do. You may not be able to play the piano or sing in the choir (neither can I), but you can be good at doing something. It may be that your greatest abilities are found in areas outside the church. Some pastors' wives are career women. Whether this would work for you is something only you, God, and your husband can decide. Applying biblical principles at this point can be difficult. We tend to interpret them through our own lens, according to what works best for us in a given situation.

A friend of mine, whose husband pastors a church of over 4,000, works part time. She says she does so because it helps her by pulling her away from the constant demands of their church work. I have observed her in this and found the following: 1) She takes full advantage of her work as an extension of her own ministry. 2) The job does not infringe upon her personal testimony. 3) Her availability to the people is not in question. 4) She keeps a good visibility pattern within the church. 5) Her other involvement in the church more than compensates for the time she spends on her job.

If you do not work on a secular job and consider yourself in full-time co-pastor/partnership ministry, you may want to ask yourself these five questions:

1. What areas of the church would I consider as top priority needs?
2. Where is my greatest area of interest? Is it music, teaching, organization, secretarial?
3. How do these needs correlate with my skills?
4. What is my personal burden level for a particular ministry?
5. Are the opportunity and timing right? If not, am I willing to allow God time to work these things out of my life?

It is important in finding our "niche," and building our self-image, that we work within our "call." Don't be shoved, forced, or coerced into trying to do something simply because someone says you should. Most of us make our greatest mistakes in life when we agree to involve ourselves in jobs for which we are not qualified, have no burden, and simply have no interest in doing. If you can accept yourself as a person, you can also define your role under God, and let people around you learn to appreciate you for what you are. This is not meant to imply that you will never do those things you don't feel qualified to do; rather, I would encourage you to develop those areas God is calling you into.

Circumstances, needs, and lack of personnel will dictate some deviation from the "one thing" of your calling. My daughter, Deanna, a pastor's wife, chose to answer her questionnaire by sharing her feelings with me on tape. Their church had grown more rapidly than their finances, putting her in what she calls "a temporary holding pattern." She is the choir director, an organizational chairperson, and teacher of an adult Bible class. She has also made her position very clear: "This is only temporary, because my burden and call lie in the teaching field." In the meantime, her goals are being directed toward a specialized area of teaching.

In chapter 8 of my book, *Be the Woman You Want to Be,*[4] I ask the question: Can you be the woman you were meant to be? I also deal with the problem of guilt that we face when we cannot come to grips with what we are. Those three areas mentioned are: imposed guilt that others place upon us; imaginary guilt we heap upon ourselves; and the matter of sin guilt. The important thing is that we recognize our feelings for what they are and never be willing to settle for a level of mediocrity. When we are involved in too many things, we end up doing nothing well, we feel guilty about it, and are never at our best.

One of my PW friends is a great hostess. She feels this to be her ministry as she brings people together from a large spectrum of the local church body. Another of my friends is extremely active in her creative skills. She loves decorating the church for weddings, receptions, and other special occasions. That's her calling! One other person happens to enjoy her job as a janitor in a church of over 600.

[4]Ruthe White, *Be the Woman You Want to Be,* Harvest House

She does this work because, according to her, "It's reward-ing!"

The important thing is not what we do, but the spirit in which we pursue our call. When our obligations are done only out of duty, we begin to hate ourselves and resent everything and everyone, including our husbands and God.

Know What You Believe As a Person

Know what you believe as a person, not just as a pastor's wife. So much of what we do and say stems from our position as PWs. We are always thinking, "How does this apply to others?" When, and if, this attitude becomes persistent we soon find ourselves in a state of spiritual dearth.

Remember: your self-concept is strengthened when you allow God to minister to you on a personal level. You *can* allow God to speak to you! You do not have to become dependent upon your husband or his ministry to meet all your spiritual, emotional, and psychological needs. You must first open yourself up to God, be honest with him about your feelings, and let him touch you right at the point of your need. Then, and only then, will you be able to touch others in a meaningful way. The Apostle Paul often spoke to the early church about his feelings, his times of imprisonment. (And what prison is worse than the one in which many of us live, isolated from our better selves?) He wrote, "Father of mercies and God of all comfort, who comforts us in all our affliction so that we may be able to comfort those who are in any affliction, with the comfort with which we ourselves are comforted" (2 Cor. 1:3b, 4, Cambridge).

Learn How to Accept Your Personal Limitations

You can learn to accept your limitations by understanding that all talents and abilities are relevant. No woman, saint or sinner, is blessed with everything. You, as a woman, must learn to live within the framework of what God has given you.

(Let us never forget, we as PWs may have problems of self-worth, but they don't always stem from our husbands' work. We do bring a lot of this psychological "baggage" into the ministry with us.) If you have a low opinion of yourself and your ability you probably had it long before you met your husband. Not only so, you would do well to recognize that you are not the only person in the world struggling with self-identity. True, because of the work you are engaged in, you are more vulnerable than some who have secular professions. It may be, however, that your sense of worthlessness is accelerated because you see so much that needs to be done in such a short period of time. You feel the urgency of your task as you look toward Christ's second coming.

Accepting your limitations also means that you can come to grips with your role as a pastor's wife without resentment toward it. You and I dare not point our fingers at the church and blame the congregation for all the traumas that come into our lives; nor can we say, "The church makes me feel this way." If you permit yourself to be stripped of your self-worth you cannot lay the blame at the foyer of the church sanctuary.

Eleanor Roosevelt was not the most beautiful woman of her day. In fact, she was called the "ugly duckling" by some of her peers. Whether you like her political philosophy or not, you must admit she was a woman of great courage. It was she who once said, "No one can make you feel inferior unless you allow them to."

A twenty-two-year-old female university student once wrote to the clinical psychologist, Dr. Loriene Chase,[5] about a problem of feeling rejected by her family. It seems that her sisters, who were much larger than she, were always buying clothes for her in *their* sizes. They minimized the work she was doing as a ballet dancer by saying, "Standing on your toes is so simple." When she asked Dr. Chase

[5] *Westways* magazine, "Casebook of Dr. Chase," May 1982

how to deal with the problem she was given some guidelines on how she could better understand herself in relation to her own accomplishments. The college student was encouraged to do the following:

1. Understand that while she was trying to rise above the level of mediocrity found in her family, she was, nevertheless, being immobilized in her behavior because of her great need for their approval. The student was warned that it was highly possible for her emotional dependency to outweigh her desire to follow her own destiny.

2. Those who were the detractors from her acceptance were also the authors of her motivation, leading her away from her dependence upon them.

3. She was asked to conquer the reaction toward those persons who were negative in her life, by looking at the internal cause of her emotional state.

While Loriene Chase's article was not written from a biblical stance, it is worth our consideration. She said, "Let us consider that no one thing has any power over us that we do not allow."

GROWTH PLAN

1. Are you usually happy?

   Do you know that happiness is the way you interpret life?

2. Can you cope with your problems as they arise?

   Can you actively attack the problem and deal with it?

3. Do you have an insight into your own weaknesses?

   Balance in life provides you with the ability to look at yourself more objectively.

4. Are you engaged in a work you enjoy?

   "Burnout" comes from overworry rather than being overworked.

5. Do you live life with zest?

Laughter is the window of the soul and humor is the glass that reflects it outwardly.

Suggested Reading:

Berry, Jo, *Priscilla Principle: Making Your Life a Ministry*, Broadman

Chambers, Oswald, *Still Higher for His Highest*, Zondervan

Coble, Betty J., *Private Life of a Minister's Wife*, Broadman

MacDonald, Gail, *High Call, High Privilege*, Tyndale

Montgomery, Shirley E., *Growth Guide for Ministers' Wives*, Broadman

Nelson, Martha, *This Call We Share*, Broadman

Senter, Ruth, *So You're the Pastor's Wife*, Zondervan

. . . you yourself must be an example to them of good deeds of every kind. Let everything you do reflect your love of the truth and the fact that you are in dead earnest about it.

TITUS 2:7 (TLB)

FIVE

You, the Role Model

GOD DOES NOT ASK US,

AS SPIRITUAL ROLE

MODELS, TO GO OUT

AND REPRODUCE

OURSELVES IN OTHERS.

INSTEAD, HE COMMIS-

SIONS US TO ALLOW

HIMSELF TO BE REPRO-

DUCED IN US!

Across the aisle from me, in a Lake Arrowhead, California, restaurant, sat a late-twentyish-looking couple. The young man and woman were discussing, in rather loud tones, the prevailing drug problems of the Hollywood set. When their meal and mine were finished we all walked out to our cars together. Standing outside the door, I could see they were in a chatting mood. Having overheard bits of their previous conversation, I was curious about their opinions.

"Pardon me," I said. "I couldn't help hearing a part of your conversation. Tell me something. Why do you feel

we are having such a growing drug problem?"

The sophisticated young man looked me in the eye, and with pathos in his voice, said: "Lady, we have no role models in our society. If you would like to do something to help us, tell the older generation to provide us with some positive role models. We need someone to show us the way."

Show us the way!

Those words rang through my ears until my heart pounded. I was reminded of the Ethiopian to whom the Angel of the Lord sent the Apostle Philip. The man, a treasurer under authority of Queen Candace, was sitting in his chariot reading aloud from the scroll of Isaiah.

Philip, having overheard him reading, asked, "Do you understand it?"

"How can I when there is no one to instruct me?" the man answered (Acts 8:31, TLB).

We are warned in Matthew's Gospel (15:14) lest we become as the blind who are guiding the blind, so that both fall into the ditch. There is nothing more devastating to God's kingdom than blind leadership: ministers, wives, and others whose lives are tainted with indiscretion, whose financial dealings are shady, and whose life-styles are flagrantly questionable.

The position of leadership brings with it some discretionary codes of conduct. We are responsible to protect ourselves from those things that carry the "appearance of evil." Our outer conduct reflects our values as *persons,* our abilities to do the *tasks* God has called us to, and the *cost* we must pay to be our best for him.

You, the Person within Your Role

May you never lose sight of the person within your role! The job you have been called to do is a personal one. You as an individual are responsible for your own actions. Let us reconsider the words of Paul to the Thessalonians (1 Thess. 5:22), urging them to abstain from those things that appeared to be evil. In verse 13 of chapter 5 Paul gave instructions to the church regarding their attitude toward those in the ministry. He urged the people to esteem the ministers highly and in love. Then he followed that statement with fourteen commands to Christians in view of Christ's second coming.

The entire concept of his teaching is capsulized in the command for abstention. (Note: What those evils were, he did not reveal.) Without getting negative in this regard, we might look at what God calls evil. Scripture teaches us about corrupt thoughts, eyes and hearts that lust, conversations that are unchristian, a covetous spirit, and quibbling jealousy. It gives them all one label: evil!

As a PW, you will seek to guard your character. Your character is what you are, while your reputation is what people say you are! You can't always keep people from talking about you, and a positive reputation is to be valued. But your personal character, the real you, should be held in the highest esteem. That is the person with whom you eat and sleep and face life daily! So be true to that inner principle of life. As a pastor's wife, I urge you to build yourself up in the faith, knowing that growth and intrinsic values are not the products of instant growth. Watch out for anything in which you may be involved that would cause people to question your honesty or morality, and walk with God. As a person in leadership, ask yourself:

1. What kind of *person* am I, and can I live with the person I am?
2. Am I a getter or a giver? (Remember, there are two kinds of people in the world, the "getters" and the "givers"—those who are in their positions of leadership because of what they expect to get out of it, and those who seek to give.)
3. Am I negative or positive in my attitude? (A negative individual spreads a negative feeling.)
4. Am I toxic or nontoxic in my personality? (Some people

make others feel they are a better person because of having met them; others bring about the opposite reaction.)

5. Am I a user of people or am *I* willing to be used for the kingdom's sake?

Regardless of where you are at the moment, you are the result of what you have been. The real person behind what you do and say is governed by the character principle of your life. (In my book, *Today's Woman: In Search of Freedom,*[6] I deal with this subject at length.) As a leader, your actions will be emulated by those around you, the people whose lives you touch daily.

I need not remind you of the scarcity of good role models. There are always too few. Each generation needs its own heroes, persons to whom they can look up, leaders to admire—including ministers' wives. The challenge for role models reaches into all segments of our society, and the demand of our day is great. We do have a responsibility to fulfill and a task to perform.

Your Task As a Role Model

Your task is a universal one, and it is twofold. You are being called to make disciples, and to teach. We are asked not only to duplicate, but to multiply. That can only be done as we grow through what we have learned from those who are faithful to the Word, and then pass it on to others. This is the way of *example*. It is said that someone once asked Einstein, the great scientist, how to raise children. He replied, "By example, example, example."

A girl came to my husband's office for counseling. Her mother had voiced her concern to us about her daughter's lack of interest in spiritual things. When the girl called and asked for an appointment to speak with my husband, we were all pleased.

[6]Ruthe White, *Today's Woman: In Search of Freedom,* Harvest House

"Pastor, you want to know why I don't attend church? I'll tell you why! My mother is your organist. She has been sitting on that organ stool for years. I am now eighteen; in my entire lifetime I have never seen my mother reading her Bible, or found her on her knees in prayer. I don't want the kind of religion my mother has."

The greatest task we have is in being a living example. A missionary once told the story of having spent years at a mission station teaching the natives. They had built a mission school on the compound. One day while the missionary and his family were out of town, their house burned to the ground. Nothing was saved. When the missionary returned with his family he found the remains of all their earthly belongings in an ash heap. Standing around, looking on, were the students he had taught. Knowing that he had spoken with them about his own faith and trust in God, he was aware that they would be looking for his response to this situation.

The missionary told of how his family wept with horror as they viewed the debris that lay stretched out before them. He spoke of his own feelings as he mustered the courage to open the car door and step into the pile of waste. When he reached what once had been their family living room, he knelt in the ashes and prayed, "God, I have always trusted you and I trust you now!" When he rose from his knees he found the students kneeling also. They had just witnessed a living, visual example of what the man had taught.

Our task is definable because it is a clear-cut command: Go and teach! We are not called to teach our theories, the latest Christian fadism, or philosophical ideas; we are to teach the Word! The process of teaching, whether by example of life and/or through verbal means, is very much like the work of the farmer. Our mission, like that of the man who farms, is to plant the seed. The germination, and its reproduction, are not ours, but God's. It is God who produces the harvest of our labors. He brings the work of our hands to its fruition. To entrust, or plant, that which we have learned means that we must relinquish our rights to hold onto it. We deposit it into the life of someone else!

One of the greatest thrills that has come to me occurred when my phone rang not long ago. Kathy Rider, a young Christian, called to say she was now teaching a ladies' Bible class. For years Kathy had sat in my women's classes with her pencil and paper in hand—she rarely missed a session of our weekly study. When Kathy spoke with me she was exuberant:

> I am here at home going through five years of your notes. These were taken while you and your husband were ministering in our church. Looking through these in preparation for my own classes, I was reminded of you. . . . I just want you to know I'm teaching what you taught me.

At that moment my mind rushed back as I asked myself, *"Did you teach Kathy something that was teachable?"* There was a sense of satisfaction that came to me in knowing I had, to the best of my ability, adhered to the biblical concepts as I knew them and as they governed my own life. For that reason, I was unafraid for her to reproduce them in others.

My husband, Claude, has a saying: "You had best be careful what you teach. You will not only be expected to live by it, it will come back to you in time." Knowing this obligates us to the *task* of teaching sound doctrine and understanding the *cost* of doing so.

The Cost of Role Modeling

It does and will cost you something to be a spiritual role model. The price of true discipleship does not come with a "markdown" sales tag attached. You will find there is a cost involved in time, energy, and finances! It may mean that you, like the Good Samaritan, will have to invest in someone's future.

Chuck Swindoll, in his book, *Improving Your Serve*,[7] deals with this subject in a direct manner. He wrote:

> *Following Christ as his disciple is a costly, unselfish decision. It calls for a radical examination of our self-centered life-styles.*
>
> *Self-denial is not a popular theme in our church circles. How many times lately have you heard the old hymn: "Must Jesus bear the cross alone and all the world go free? No, there's a cross for everyone and there's a cross for me."*

That idea has been almost an anathema, a curse, in the minds of many twentieth-century leaders. We want the prestige, big cars, designer clothes, and all the glory of an up-front ministry; but let us guard our motives to make sure we are not getting these at the expense of required moments of sacrifice, the *cost* of discipleship!

GROWTH PLAN

Plan of participation:
1. List the names of persons who have influenced your life in a most positive way.
2. List three qualities in the life of those individuals who made the greatest input into your life.
3. List areas of your own life.

STRONG POINTS   NEED HELP

[7]Charles Swindoll, *Improving Your Serve: The Art of Unselfish Living,* Word Books

Identify those areas where you need help and present them to God. He has promised to help you! (See James 1:5.)

Suggested Reading:
Mostrom, Donald C., *Intimacy with God,* Tyndale

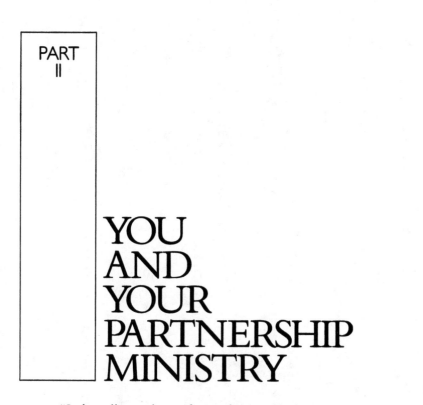

PART
II

YOU
AND
YOUR
PARTNERSHIP
MINISTRY

"I also tell you this—if two of you agree down here on earth concerning anything you ask for, my Father in heaven will do it for you."
MATTHEW 18:19 (TLB)

SIX

You and Your Pastor Husband

OUR HUSBANDS

WANT US TO RESPECT

THEM FOR WHO THEY

ARE INSTEAD OF FOR

WHAT THEY DO.

When the young evangelist, who later became my husband, rolled into town driving his spiffy, chrome-trimmed black Chevrolet, he turned the head of every young single woman in our church (a few outside, too). It can be said he brought a spiritual awakening to the women of our community as they suddenly became aware of their eternal and marital destiny!

We met in late January for the first time, began dating shortly after, and he proposed to me three months later. Thoughts of becoming the wife of such a successful young preacher buoyed my spirits during the long summer months of preparation for our wedding day. While I worked hard at making sure every wedding detail was carefully organized, there were other areas of my future life for which I could not plan.

I had not anticipated the reaction of some of our friends toward our engagement. Claude's buddies thought he was getting cheated because they knew I didn't play the piano or sing. "Everyone knows a preacher's wife is supposed to be talented in the music field," they would say to him. So his admirers would try to set him up with some gal who could offer him a neat little musical package. On the other hand, there were friends of mine who insisted I was getting the lesser deal. "After all, Ruthe, why do you want to marry a dying man?" they would ask me. He had contracted a strain of malaria while in the South Pacific, and the infection which had almost taken his life was still active in his system. His skin was yellow from medication, and he looked frail even to me. Despite the unsolicited advice that was coming to us, we went ahead with our wedding plans and were married on September 1 of that same year.

Little did I know that less than one week after our marriage, Claude would be rushed to a local pastor's home, too weak to keep his scheduled speaking appointment. My emotions were running the gamut between love and fear. There was the love I felt for the man I had just wed, and the fear of marrying "a dying man," as some of my friends had warned me. While kneeling beside his bed, feeling helpless, watching as he thrashed the covers in a fitful sleep, the agony of my hurt faced the cold realism of what could happen.

"God, what do I do next?" I cried out in desperation.

My thoughts and prayers turned to panic as I reached out to touch Claude's hand. When I took hold of his sweaty palm I knew he was sicker than any of us had thought. With no money to hospitalize him, there was little I could do but call out to God for his help. The Lord did come to our aid. The very next morning Claude was able to get out of bed and keep his day's speaking assignment. (The interesting fact is that, since that time—over twenty-five years ago—he has had no malarial symptoms.)

Those were difficult moments in our lives. Our marriage

relationship was tested, our love tried. We knew that if our marriage and ministry were to be successful we had to make each other the number one priority of our lives. Even knowing that brought some conflict. I wondered, *What is my responsibility toward him? Toward myself? How am I to implement the compelling desire of my heart to be a good pastor's wife? Is there anyone, anywhere, who can help me?*

My first rude awakening came in trying to assume the privileged obligation of first being his wife. I was not, am not, nor ever shall be that perfect wife role model. (I wonder if there is such a thing?) I could not foresee, therefore I could not plan for those moments down the road when my husband would need me most. As a result, there were times when I did not recognize his emotional, psychological, and physical needs as readily as I might have. (I may have been too busy doing the "Lord's work" to be totally aware or conscious of his needs.) As time taught me to become more sensitive to his personal needs, the learning process evolved into an attitude: one of willingness to cooperate with him in his work, communicate my feelings to him, and let him share his with me. To do this required my making a direct effort to better understand my responsibility toward him. Through the struggle I discovered some levels of need that seem to be an integral part of a minister husband's psychological makeup.

Our Husbands Need Our Support and Cooperation

One thing my husband considers necessary to his own well-being is the knowledge that a trusting relationship exists between us. He and I both know there are times when I have to trust him and be willing to cooperate with him, even when I do not understand what is going on. We also know we cannot predict those moments when he might be asked to do something or be with someone that would require blind faith on my part and a trusting, cooperative attitute toward his work. His knowing that we are voluntarily seeking to unite our mental, spiritual, and physical energies, and that

I trust him, free him to carry out the responsibilities of our ministry more effectively.

In order to do this we both had to learn what it meant to be flexible, to give and take, as we tried to establish a base for mutual trust. We came to understand that there could be no unity in our marriage without first becoming active participants in the other's belief system. While growing together we also had to become aware of those things the other person felt was important. This learning process did not come overnight. But, as we have learned together, it has brought us to a place of agreement in purpose, a better understanding of each other, a commitment to work on our common goals, and a trusting relationship. Trusting meant we had to learn mutual understanding and cooperation.

Your Husband Needs Intimacy in Companionship

Your husband needs to know that you support him and that he can depend upon you for companionship. Webster's dictionary defines the word "companion" as "an associate, comrade, a pair or set of like things, a person employed to live or travel with another and act in the capacity of a friend." When your husband can feel you are his best friend, both of you know you have reached a place of mature growth. A friendship-comrade relationship between a spouse and partner is not one of carbon-copy interests. It simply means that one has learned to appreciate what is liked in the other person and to tolerate, with Christian virtue, those things disliked. That is companionship—friendship and trust!

As the wife of a clergyman you will want to make sure you do not betray that cooperative trust. You dare not contradict, or by your actions demonstrate that you are in opposition to your husband's decisions. What you say to him in the privacy of your own home is a different matter. (Finding the opportunity to say it is the problem. Either the kids are around, the phone rings, a parishioner drops in, there is no time, he's preaching in the morning, a "guilt

trip" takes over, or something else keeps you from address-
a problem.) Once you have discussed the situation and
closed the parsonage door, you also need to put a lock on
your mouth. If you don't discuss your arguments with
other people they won't know you have them!

Your Husband Needs You to Communicate with Him

*Communication involves good listening procedures: You listen
when you don't feel like it, don't have the time, and just don't
want to.* You cannot enjoy the benefits of companionship
with your mate unless both of you are willing to communicate about your common needs. How?

Learn to listen with your heart. A minister friend of ours,
Dwight McLauglin, often stops during one of his sermons
and, turning to his audience, asks, "Are you people listening
with your hearts?" We would all do well to stop and question whether our hearts are really listening. Can we emote,
feel, empathize with what our spouses are saying to us?
Most importantly, have our hearts grasped the impact of
what they are *trying* to tell us?

Mary, the mother of Jesus, is a beautiful example of
being a "heart listener." Luke, the biblical physician, writes
about her:

> *Mary was greatly troubled at his words and wondered what
> kind of greeting this might be (Luke 1:29, NIV).*

There are times in partnership ministry when you, like
Mary, will need to listen for more than you are hearing.
Listen for cues, those things that are important to your
husband as a person, not just as a minister. To hear him is
not always to remind him of what is best for his ministry.
Inquire about his goals for the coming year, talk about his
ambitions, seek to discover whether you are in agreement
and working toward a common cause.

Learn to listen with your ears. It is easy to turn your spouse
off mentally because you are preoccupied with other mat-

ters. In doing this you tend to respond only to those portions of the conversation that you hear. Consequently, what is being said is not always heard, nor interpreted, in the way it was intended. This breaks down the response mechanism. No one can communicate properly until he first has learned to listen well. Jesus spoke of those who, having ears, did not hear. How many times have we all been guilty of passing over another's needs simply because we have not allowed our ears to hear what that person's heart was saying?

Learn to listen with your physical self. One of the most difficult adjustments in my marriage that I have had to work on is taking time to listen. You may have the same tendency as I, to keep moving while your spouse is trying to talk with you. Many of us, as PWs, are caught in this trap; because our minds are filled with duties of the day, we pass by our mates like "flags waving in the wind." As a result of this preoccupation with our work, some parsonages are becoming little more than hotels or service stations—places to "fill up," change our clothes, and sleep. We must guard against this busyness lest we become emotional strangers and lose psychological contact with the person who feeds at our table, sleeps in our bed, and is our pastor on Sunday.

How long has it been since you took time to sit down and listen to what your husband was saying? Can you do so without interrupting his conversation or interjecting your "own pearls of wisdom"? These are important questions that deserve thoughtful answers. I am a person who does a lot of brainstorming. I listen for ideas or seek some mental solution to a problem. Sometimes ideas are not what my husband needs at that moment. What he really wants is for me to lay down my pen and pencil, or whatever else I may be doing, and just sit there without saying a word.

Good listening techniques do not come automatically. I would be the first to admit that it is not easy to sit doing nothing, when there are a million tasks begging to be finished, or when you are hearing for the "umpteenth" time how Brother Pinch Penny will not let your husband purchase new light bulbs for the church. But listen anyway! Just knowing you care, that he can trust you with his emotions, and that he enjoys your fellowship makes him feel better, and you too! So it may be that you, like me, will need to work on this point of personality development. Discovering some of the deterrents to good listening has been helpful to me. You may want to consider them also. Listed below are just four of the methods we all use at some time during the listening process: we take mental detours; tend to debate the issues we are hearing; discuss the problems internally; and get caught up in daydreaming about other things.

Detour:

While our husbands are talking about the church, we are thinking about the children, of what we will serve for dinner, or of doing the laundry.

Debate:

He says the church should be painted green and we are way ahead of him, ready to fight the issue, and gathering our arguments against what is being said.

Discussion:

We listen while mentally deciding how to top the discussion.

Dreamer: (Let's go to Yosemite . . . to Sea) . . . World.)

Caught up in our mental side-trips, we are dreaming about our next vacation or some fun trip we have planned.

Your communication level is a vital line in your marriage relationship. You will find during those times when you and your spouse are struggling with difficulties that it is important to listen and communicate your feelings to each other. For, no matter how much we try, there will be moments when we feel apprehensive about our spouse's work. But if we have learned to listen, we can feel free to talk about our feelings and emotional needs. So let's keep on listening, making sure the communication lines are open!

Dr. Richard Foth, President of Bethany College, Santa Cruz, California, recently spoke to a group of PWs at Campus Crusade in San Bernardino, California. In his sermon he gave us some suggestions as to how we could best listen to our husband's needs:

1. Take an interest in his world.
2. Put yourself in the position of a learner because it validates you and his work.
3. Don't allow yourself to be used, but do be supportive in what is important to him.
4. Never try to be his conscience.
5. Take responsibility for the manner in which you communicate with him.
6. Assume personal responsibility for your own actions by accepting the truth of what you hear.
7. Never try playing the "blame game."
8. Watch your language. (The word "love" can be worn out. Be careful how you use it. It can be much like an accordian that stretches out too far.)
9. Use words in communicating that cause a mutual reaction of caring, such as, "I trust, respect, and admire you."
10. Give him to God every day.

Christian love, we must remember, seeks to fulfill rather than to be fulfilled. It is a love that we teach to others; but we have to work to maintain it in our own marriages, even while living in the parsonage.

GROWTH PLAN

1. Consider ways in which you can build your husband's image with your parishioners:

   a) _____

   b) _____

   c) _____

2. Tell your husband three reasons for feeling you can trust him:

   a) _____

   b) _____

   c) _____

3. Give him three reasons you respect him; be specific:

   a) _____

   b) _____

   c) _____

4. Promise yourself that you will make a conscious effort to:
   a) Never denigrate or criticize him in front of others.
   b) Respect his masculinity by not becoming competitive or argumentative in the presence of others.
   c) Show by gestures that you genuinely respect him and enjoy the companionship the two of you share.

5. Do not seek to become the dominant person in the relationship or leave the impression with people that you are the authority figure in the home.

Suggested Reading:

Augsburger, David, *Caring Enough to Confront*, Regal Books

Hardisty, Margaret, *Your Husband and Your Emotional Needs*, Harvest House

LaHaye, Beverly and Tim, *The Act of Marriage*, Zondervan

Smedes, Lewis B., *Love within Limits: A Realistic View of I Corinthians 13*, Eerdmans

Welter, Paul, *The Family: Stronger after Crisis*, Tyndale

Wright, Norman H., *Communication: Key to Your Marriage*, Regal Books

Wright, Norman H., *The Pillars of Marriage*, Regal Books

Wright, Norman H., *Seasons of a Marriage*, Regal Books

SOME QUESTIONS FOR YOU AND YOUR HUSBAND TO DISCUSS TOGETHER

MINISTERS' WIVES IN ACTION

	YES	NO
1. If your phone were to ring during your evening meal and the person calling asked to speak to your husband, would you:		
a. Call him to the phone immediately?	___	___
b. Inquire if the call was an emergency and offer to have your husband return the call after he finished his evening meal?	___	___
c. Speak to the caller yourself and give him all the information he needs?	___	___
2. If your husband left the office at an agreed time, could he be reasonably sure when he arrived home that you would have dinner ready?	___	___
3. Do you have one night a week that is marked off the church calendar designed "just for the family"?	___	___
4. If you had one night you scheduled to spend with the family and someone called inviting you to go somewhere, would you be apt to go out rather than staying home?	___	___
5. If you have children, can they expect dinner to be served at the same time each day?	___	___

		YES	NO

6. Do you eat your evening meals within one hour of the same time of day at least four days a week?   ____ ____

7. Are you involved with your husband in church work on an average of more than two nights a week, excluding the weekends?   ____ ____

8. Are you personally responsible for more than one area of ministry within your church?   ____ ____

9. Do you make many hospital calls with your husband?   ____ ____

10. Do your church women feel free to drop in on you just any time?   ____ ____

11. If you were entertaining friends outside the church and some of your husband's parishioners dropped by to visit, would you:
   a. Meet them at the door and encourage them by telling them how welcome they are?   ____ ____
   b. Be kind, but inform them you have guests and inquire if you can talk with them at a later time?   ____ ____
   c. Invite them in to eat with you?   ____ ____

12. Do your church ladies know that you have a certain time set aside each day for your own personal devotions, and that you prefer no phone calls during that time?   ____ ____

13. If someone accused you of spending too much time with your children's activities would you:

                                                                   YES   NO

    a. Explain why you are doing that? ____ ____

    b. Listen, smile, and forget all about it? ____ ____

    c. Feel guilty for neglecting some area of the church to take care of the children's needs? ____ ____

14. Do you discuss church problems of any kind in the presence of your children? ____ ____

15. When you and your husband are alone do you spend a major part of your time discussing things pertaining to the church? ____ ____

16. Do you take time to make special occasions SPECIAL for your family—such as Valentine's Day, birthdays, Thanksgiving, and any other holidays? ____ ____

17. Do you often feel you have too much to do? ____ ____

18. If someone came to you complaining about something your husband had done, would you:

    a. Defend his position? ____ ____

    b. Encourage the person to speak directly to your husband? ____ ____

    c. Assure the person that you will speak to your husband about the matter? ____ ____

19. When you buy something new do you have a tendency to apologize to your church women about it? ____ ____

		YES	NO
20.	If complimented by someone about something you are wearing, can you accept it without feeling you need to explain how much you paid for it?	___	___
21.	Do you openly disagree with your husband in the presence of other women?	___	___
22.	Can you counsel other women without sharing with them any personal problems you might have, such as those related to your sex life?	___	___
23.	Do you discuss your husband's weaknesses with any of the church women?	___	___
24.	Are you generally seen in public socializing with basically the same few women in your congregation?	___	___
25.	Do you often find yourself resenting your husband's work?	___	___

PARSONS IN ACTION

		YES	NO
1.	Do you usually call your wife when you know an appointment is going to keep you later than she expects?	___	___
2.	If you had an agreement to take your wife out to dinner and someone called demanding an appointment, would you: a. Call your wife and explain where you were going and promise to take her out next week?	___	___

		YES	NO

b. After determining there was no emergency on the part of the caller, would you tell the person you had a previous appointment and agree to speak with him at another time? ____ ____

c. Figure it didn't really matter whether you contacted your wife or not, since she probably wouldn't be ready anyway? ____ ____

3. Do you come home from the church office within the same hour of each day at least four days out of the week? ____ ____

4. Can your wife be reasonably sure you will be home to eat at the designated dinner hour? ____ ____

5. Do you make an effort to be sure your wife is properly introduced when she accompanies you to a ministerial function? ____ ____

6. Is your wife given the opportunity to decorate her home and/or the parsonage in any manner she chooses? ____ ____

7. Do you, as a man, have a tendency to question her ability to choose a color or style of furniture as it relates to the home? ____ ____

8. If your church gave you a Christmas gift of $500, would you:
a. Give your wife half? ____ ____
b. Agree together with your wife about how it should be spent? ____ ____

		YES	NO
c.	Feel that it was yours and count it into the budget?	—	—
9.	Do you make your wife the brunt of your jokes?	—	—
10.	Do you laugh at your wife's mistakes in the presence of others?	—	—
11.	Can you show affection toward your wife openly without feeling embarrassed?	—	—
12.	Do you feel your ministry comes before anything else?	—	—
13.	Can you take off one night each week for the family without "giving in" when someone calls?	—	—
14.	If you planned an evening with your family and a board member called demanding to see you, could you say "No" to him, providing there was no emergency?	—	—
15.	Do you have a time of day that your church people know is set aside for prayer and study?	—	—
16.	If someone called during your study time would you have a tendency to speak with the person?	—	—
17.	Do you spend more evenings away from home than at home?	—	—

18. If you were playing a game with your child and a church member showed up at your house unexpectedly, would you: YES   NO

    a. Invite him in?

    b. Ask what you might do for him and encourage the person to make an appointment with you at your office?

    c. Tell the person he is not interrupting anything important and send the child to pick up his toy?

19. Do you feel your wife is an extension of your ministry?

20. Would you prefer your wife to be less involved in the church?

21. Would you prefer your wife to be more involved in the church?

22. Do you take your wife out for an evening alone on an average of at least once each month?

23. If someone criticized your wife would you:

    a. Expect her to defend herself?

    b. Let the person know you did not appreciate the comment?

    c. Agree with the person and tell him you will take the matter up with her?

24. Do you ask your wife to do more than you ask of other women in your congregation (as related to church responsibility)?

25. Do you feel your wife is jealous of your relationship and time spent in counseling other women in church-related work?

YES   NO

___   ___

. . . and little children don't pay for their father's and mother's food—it's the other way around; parents supply food for their children.
2 CORINTHIANS 12:14b (TLB)

SEVEN

You and Your Child

OUR TOs (THEOLOGICAL

OFFSPRING) HURT

WITH US, AND WHEN

WE FEEL REJECTED,

THEY DO ALSO.

One of the greatest fears I experienced as a pastor's wife was that of losing my own two daughters while trying to help everyone else's children. I was afraid that even if I did all I could, my own children might become disillusioned by the "fishbowl" in which they lived, perhaps never wanting to serve God in a meaningful way.

We are not alone in our struggles with the responsibilities of home, family, church—and especially the great concern we share for our children. Every clergy parent has, at some time, been reminded of another preacher's kid who was maladjusted and broke all the rules of Christian behavior. (You can be sure if there ever has been such a kid you will hear about it.) We, as parents, live in fear of what *might* happen to our child. We also know that just because our

TOs live in houses owned by the church, and their fathers are their pastors, those things in themselves do not exempt them from life.

Some things are certain—our parsonage families are not without conflict and everything in our homes is not always "just perfect" (though sometimes we try to make people believe it is). We, like everyone else, must work at rearing our children. In the process, neither we nor our kids will get through life without making some mistakes. We will disappoint our TOs—and they us! Our kids will not be able to please all the church people, either. Sometimes we want our children to be perfect so they can make us look good.

It took me a long time to learn that my girls didn't *have* to be clean, starched, and ruffled twenty-four hours a day; the house didn't *have* to be immaculate on a minute's notice; and those who lived there didn't *have* to be without human error. Sure, it is embarrassing when one of our kids pulls a "shenanigan" on us. As mothers, we shudder at the thought of "what our child might do next." We have all known moments of parental panic when our patience was tried to the limit.

I remember the time when my (then) not quite-three-year-old Deanna got the paint bucket and proceeded with brush in hand to color the front church steps a crimson red. And when my other daughter requested prayer in her Sunday school class: "Pray for my mommy; she is going to have another baby. Please don't bother to put my name on the roll book 'cause my daddy won't be stayin' at this church long."

The truth of the matter was we had just accepted the pastorate of the church and that was our first Sunday there. We had not yet moved into the parsonage, and I wasn't pregnant! Our five-year-old Jan had thrown the church ladies into a "tizzy." I was shocked to find, upon moving into the parsonage, that one bedroom had suddenly been decorated with a nursery motif. Months later I discovered what Jan had told the woman.

I also found out that none of those little things my children did were going to make a great deal of difference in our lives in the long run. I, as a clergy parent, had to change the focus of my goal from raising perfect children to the *ultimate* purpose of my life: the important task of bringing my children to a personal relationship with Jesus Christ.

Unequivocally, our first aim should be to provide our children with an example they can emulate, giving them tools to implement their spiritual growth, and working to help them achieve their personal life goals. We can never assume that because we are in the Lord's work our children will automatically come to know him. There seem to be two coexisting attitudes on the part of parsonage parents. First, there is the PW who tends to feel her child doesn't have a chance in life—because of the church people, where the family lives, and what they do. There seems always to be a prevailing spirit of negativism that rests upon the household because of those fears. A recent article in *Partnership* magazine (a bimonthly periodical geared to the needs of the woman in partnership ministry), hopefully did a lot to assuage the apprehensions of PWs raising children in the parsonage.

Vicki T. deVries, in her research for the *Partnership* article, shows that the clergy child is no worse off, and in some cases is better off, than the nonclergy kid. She says our TOs tend to feel good about themselves, to have open relationships with their fathers, to be adept in verbal skills, and to acquire an early understanding of spiritual values. When she asked pastors' wives about their children's social development, they ranked their TOs as being "very well" or "well" adjusted to society.

Second, there are also those PWs who act as if their children are without fault and never do anything wrong. They place them on a level of superiority above other kids

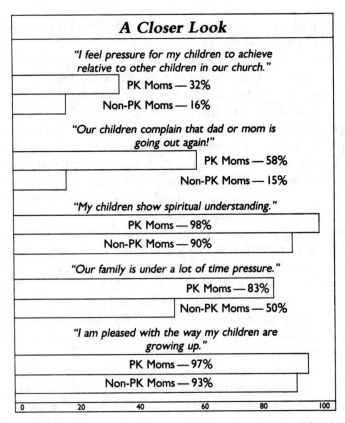

A Closer Look

"I feel pressure for my children to achieve relative to other children in our church."

PK Moms — 32%

Non-PK Moms — 16%

"Our children complain that dad or mom is going out again!"

PK Moms — 58%

Non-PK Moms — 15%

"My children show spiritual understanding."

PK Moms — 98%

Non-PK Moms — 90%

"Our family is under a lot of time pressure."

PK Moms — 83%

Non-PK Moms — 50%

"I am pleased with the way my children are growing up."

PK Moms — 97%

Non-PK Moms — 93%

0   20   40   60   80   100

Partnership *magazine, September/October 1984, "Pastors' Wives Take a Look at Their Kids," Vicki T. deVries*

in the church. The PWs' assumption seems to be that, by virtue of who the parents are, the child will always do the proper thing. More importantly, they seem to believe their TOs are born as little saints.

We dare not assume either of these views. To do so abdicates our responsibility toward both God and the child. To feel that our kids haven't a chance in life is to blame God for our problems. To say they are going to grow up to be mature Christians because of our being in the Lord's work is to make God the "fall guy." Our children are ours to teach, to train, and to nurture. We cannot leave all the training and spiritual guidance to members of the church staff. That is our responsibility! Moses, in the Old Testament, gave a command to the people of Israel about teaching their children. He told them:

> O Israel, listen: Jehovah is our God, Jehovah alone. You must love him with all your heart, soul, and might. And you must think constantly about these commandments I am giving you today. You must teach them to your children and talk about them when you are at home or out for a walk; at bedtime and the first thing in the morning. Tie them on your finger, wear them on your forehead, and write them on the doorposts of your house! (Deut. 6:4-9, TLB).

I can hear some of you saying, "No way!" But, wait a minute. I don't believe God expects us to be preaching machines who are always sermonizing our kids (though I am sometimes guilty of doing this). He does want us to keep his precepts always before our children. Personally, I am not one of those mothers who feels that the only way to witness is by plastering the living room walls with religious mottoes. To me that can easily become nothing more than an external identification process, a cheap cop-out for not taking care of the weightier matter of teaching. This is particularly true if it is the only form we use for transmitting our belief systems.

None of us can predict how our TOs will respond to parsonage life or why some of our kids react toward the church as they do. However, there is some observable evidence that in those clergy homes where the children grow up to value their parents' belief systems, all the families have some things in common: 1) There is an atmosphere or environment within the home making the child feel accepted and loved; 2) social and spiritual alternatives are provided through the home; and 3) the child is given a strong self-image.

Providing Our Children
with a Spiritual Environment

An essential element for spiritual growth is found in good reading material. If you can't afford a library, take your child to the public library. Invest some of your monies in books geared to the age level of your child. Once when I was a guest in a pastor's home, the father turned to me and asked to be excused from the room for a few moments as he put his child to bed. Upon returning, he explained that he and his child were reading one of C. S. Lewis's Narnia books together.

Music is another way to provide a growing atmosphere within the home. We all know good music can be a mood-setter. Give your children records of songs with lyrics that teach Christian values. You may have to work on this one a bit, but it's worth the effort.

Special days are wonderful occasions to establish growth learning patterns. This requires a great deal of effort on our part, as mothers. The special seasons of the year are usually our busiest times. But doing little things such as putting out Valentine placemats, an Easter arrangement, or Christmas decor adds to the atmosphere of the home. It tells your child that you are interested in what goes on in the world around him. Also, by doing so, your home becomes the focal point of your child's activity. You are building memories that will linger in the mind of your child for years to come.

When I asked my daughters what they remembered most about living in the parsonage, I was surprised! They didn't talk about the gifts church people had given them. Instead, they reminded me of those special days such as Father's Day, when the dining room table was let out to serve twelve people. It was filled with our family of four, and the others were widowed men and teenagers who were brought in to help entertain them.

Daddy Mac was a family favorite. He was past seventy

when he accepted Christ as his personal Savior. Sometimes his language was not as clean as was his heart, but we loved him just the same. He would come in, sit down at our table, and begin to eat. Then he would stroke his bald head and say, "By golly, this is the best food I ever et." When the meal was finished we would all retire into the living room where the teenagers would entertain our geriatric guests.

Sometimes our special days were reserved just for us, our family. Claude would serve us communion and we would worship together. But things didn't always work out the way they were planned! There were occasions when our spiritual emphasis time was turned into a fiasco. Once, right in the middle of our devotions, our Pekingese dog, Hope, ran to the door and back to the window, barking. She was tearing up the house trying to get outside to chase our neighbor's cat. We all ended up with the giggles. The important thing was not that the solemnity of our occasion was interrupted, but that we could laugh as well as pray together.

Humor is vital to growth. As parents you need to provide a time and allow room for laughter. Humor, according to humorist Carl Reiner, is something that is learned; it is not inherited. If you don't keep some laughter around your hearth, the house will become like a morgue. The evening meal was our time to enjoy being together as a family unit. We chose that time to share our day's activities and latest anecdotes. Once our humor got us into trouble! Jan had heard a joke from someone and failed to clear it with her daddy before piping up at the dinner table. We were entertaining the bishop of our denomination that evening, when she asked him:

"Bishop, do you know what Adam said to Eve?"

"No," the bishop replied with his usual poker-faced expression.

" 'Eve, Eve,' Adam said to her, 'a leaf is missing!' "

The churchman laughed uproariously, knowing the six-year-old child had not gotten our permission to share her latest conversational findings.

Build an Atmosphere of Trust for Your Child

We cannot protect our children from all tension any more than we can keep them from knowing some things around the church we would rather they did not discover; so we must let them know we trust them. We are often caught in a quandary about how much we should, or shouldn't, tell our children. Rather than leave our TOs to surmise, or figure things out on their own, we can give them alternatives:

1. Explain to your child anything (s)he is likely to hear through another child.
2. Give out only information that is needed and that your child can understand.
3. Clear up any fantasies or false ideas that might be in your child's mind.
4. Make sure the child is trained to keep family confidences.
5. Let the child know that you trust him/her.

Build Your Child's Self-image

Because clergy children are often exposed to disgruntled church members, it is important that we keep in touch with their feelings and build within them a good self-image. Our children often catch the brunt of frustrated people who dislike something their father does. I remember when one person in a church we served came to my husband confessing infidelity in his marriage. Upon leaving the office, the man realized what he had done and hated both himself for telling, and my husband for knowing about it. He threatened our family by phone, saying he would ruin our reputation and run us out of the city. When our girls were coming home from school he would often pull up beside them and yell at them about how terrible their parents were. Sometimes we forget that our kids are capable of deep feelings and hurts. They do hurt with us, and when we are rejected they feel rejected also.

One child, upon learning that his father had been voted out of the church, wept, saying, "Why don't they like us anymore?" Our children feel rejection strongly, and it is so vitally important that they know they are accepted and loved by their parents. In another church my husband pastored, one lady would stand up right in the middle of the church service and stalk out when our girls were being featured as special singers. She just didn't like their classical style of music. Our kids struggled with that for a long time before reaching the ability to understand and accept this rejection. These things do have an effect upon the lives of our children, but we can offset some negative conditioning by giving them a good self-concept:

1. Teach them the disciplines of life.
2. Give them clear but firm guidelines from which you do not deviate. There need be only a few rules in the house if you major on the important issues instead of minor things. Be predictably sure about your children's responsibilities in the home and let them know what you expect.
3. Be consistent in your discipline and balance it with love.
4. Give them room to develop as persons and not just as pastor's kids. Never punish them with, "Do you know how this will affect our ministry?"
5. Make your children feel they are the most important persons who attend your church, and their welfare comes before your other duties.
6. Assure them they have everything needed to reach their goals in life.
7. Teach them to love people by giving them an introduction to your guests. Never leave your child standing

beside you without introducing him/her to the person with whom you are talking.

8. Teach your child respect for others by giving him/her personal affirmation.
9. Give your child room for some privacy. Don't force him/her to share personal belongings with parishioners' children who are destructive.
10. Keep in touch with your child's feelings. Know what the child is thinking, where (s)he is coming from.

When you have done all you know to do, there does come that moment when you must relinquish them to God, knowing he loves them even more than you do. Never stop believing that if we *train* our children, God will do his part!

Suggested Reading:

McBirnie, William S., *How to Motivate Your Child Toward Success*, Tyndale
Moore, Dorothy and Raymond, *Home Grown Kids*, Word
Nielson, Joseph F., *You Can Be a Better Parent*, Baker
Welter, Paul, *Learning from Children*, Tyndale
Wright, Linda Raney, *Raising Children*, Tyndale

"But don't begin until you count the cost. For who would begin construction of a building without first getting estimates and then checking to see if he has enough money to pay the bills? Otherwise he might complete only the foundation before running out of funds. And then how everyone would laugh!"
LUKE 14:28, 29 (TLB)

EIGHT

You and the Church

YOU WILL NEVER WIN

ALL OF YOUR PERSONAL

BATTLES IN LIFE, BUT

IF YOU KEEP A GOOD

ATTITUDE YOU WILL BE A

WINNER REGARDLESS

OF WHAT HAPPENS.

The air was as quiet as the moving van sitting in the driveway next to our parsonage window. Locked inside the large truck was an accumulation of all my earthly belongings. It seemed to me that this was the hundredth time (though we had had only a few pastoral changes during our twenty years of ministry) that I would be unpacking, adjusting to another church, another congregation. I found myself wishing for the same inner calmness I was feeling in the almost-serene atmosphere of California's San Joaquin Valley air. There was something about the dead quietness of that humid late spring day which was stifling me. I had been warmly welcomed by the climate, but emotionally chilled with thoughts of a new pastorate.

Moving has never been easy for me! I like to feel secure in my nest, settled with family and friends. I was no more comfortable in this transition than I had been in all the others. Like any other woman, I was concerned about the condition of my furniture, and what might be broken in this move. I thought about the elegant eighteenth-century couch my husband had bought me for a birthday gift in 1952. I knew it was packed among all the other pieces—the marble-top tables, given us by a church congregation three pastorates or so back, an antique hutch (a love gift to me) I had hauled from a Mexican lady's porch and spent hours sanding down for a new varnish job. As I looked at my fingernails, all eaten away from the harsh chemicals used in stripping the hutch, I wondered, *will it be scratched and my work prove useless?*

Parked inside the garage was our car, loaded down with the fragile mementos of ministerial years. Pages of newspaper were wrapped around the delicate glass bowl Melba Hudson, our former church secretary had given me years before her death. In the same box with Melba's bowl was a crystal pitcher I treasured. It was a Christmas gift from Ora Boone, the person who had furnished my husband with all the home-canned fig jam he could eat during a six-year pastoral stint in El Centro, California. Beside those things were several containers of bric-a-brac, none of which was of value to anyone except me!

I was thinking to myself, *Another pastorate—what will this one be like? What will be the people's response to my husband's ministry?* My thoughts were being carried with me as I walked down the hallway and into the adjoining bedroom of the new parsonage. I quickly began removing my dress to put on work clothes. Suddenly I heard the door open and could hear footsteps. A deacon, not knowing we were there, had opened the door and walked inside. I thought the man entering was my husband, so I ran up the hall to ask him something. When I looked up I found myself standing face to face with the chairman of the deacon board.

Making your debut, as the new pastor's wife, wearing nothing but your underwear is not the best possible introduction! Fortunately for me, neither the man nor his wife has ever mentioned the incident to me since.

Getting settled into a new church situation can be just plain scary. I have often wished there were some foolproof plan that we could be assured is workable. Somehow, God has so ordained it that we "work out our own salvation with fear and trembling." And in so doing each of us will, and have, made some mistakes in the pastoral adaptation process. When we do fall on our faces, the best method for dealing with our errors is to admit them, take responsibility for our actions, commit the situation to God, and forget about the past. However, during the moments of wrestling with our own shortcomings we can take hope with the Apostle Paul, who said of himself:

> *I don't mean to say I am perfect. I haven't learned all I should even yet, but I keep working toward that day when I will finally be all that Christ saved me for and wants me to be (Phil. 3:12, TLB).*

There are some guidelines that I have found helpful in my own partnership ministry, particularly as they applied to my work within the church. You may want to consider some of these before pushing the emergency button on a new assignment.

Have a Workable Attitude of Mutual Appreciation

It is most essential that we make others feel they are needed and are our equals. You will be able to do this much more effectively if you give yourself some breathing space before making any major changes in the church planning organizational structure. Learn about the people within the local church setting. Memorize as many of their names as possible; find out something about them—where the husband works, if the wife does, and general information concerning their families. The church directory should provide you with that information. If there is no such directory, make this a priority item on your list.

Develop methods for determining where your talent resources are. Many churches give out annual information sheets and ask the parishioners to fill them out. Once the data is accumulated, make sure your church has a filing system and an organizational procedure enabling you to have access to that information. After having learned what is important to the people with whom you are working, you will be able to relate to them in a meaningful way.

Many of us, as PWs, reflect an attitude of perfectionism because we feel it represents us. Therefore, *our image* must be protected. Sometimes we are not aware of our *locus standi,* or standing place, until someone shocks us into realizing how demanding we are.

Judy, a younger woman in our church, came to me one day. In her kind and gracious manner she poured her heart out to me: "Mrs. White, I don't think you need me as much as I need you. I get the feeling you are such a self-sufficient person you could get this job done without me."

Her words hit me like a bolt of lightning! I was taken aback to discover that such an impression of me had come through to her. Immediately, I set out to make some corrections in my approach to dealing with people. I did so by:

1. Making a conscious effort to involve every woman in our church in an active and personal ministry.
2. Providing training, seminars, speakers, and resource material that would aid the women in their growth processes.
3. Treating each person as an equal by letting her know she was worthy of making a positive contribution to God's work.
4. Never prejudging a person's ability by her manner or appearance.

5. Giving each person the right to make his/her own mistakes without having to give excuses.
6. Skillfully working to help each woman find her place of ministry without trying to put her in someone else's mold.
7. Showing a sincere appreciation for the efforts of each individual, without comparing the person's productivity to that of another.
8. Making sure that recognition was given to those who assisted in or were responsible for the work.
9. Being free and open with my compliments to those persons who were making an effort toward growth involvement.
10. Placing before each woman the constant challenge for growth.

Provide People with Workable Tools

It is not enough to ask people to do a job. You must provide them with the tools to implement their task. If you want your women to read more, then give them books, lend them yours, or assist them in building home libraries, if your church does not have one. Bring in specialists that will assist your people. I know some of you are asking, "But where do we get the funds to do all of this?" In one pastorate we had a large group of young parents who had come out of the drug culture. They were having problems in handling their finances and supporting their families. We arranged to have a local banker, a woman, come and teach the class. On another occasion, a math teacher from our local school who was a member of our parish taught several Sunday morning sessions to young marrieds about interest rates, mortgage costs, and the best way to purchase a home. Each year, either on Mother's Day or Father's Day, a local judge was brought in to speak to the class on parenting.

Decorators are usually more than glad to bring their talents to your church. There may even be a woman in the parish with a special creative talent for putting her home together. If so, arrange a time for your ladies to learn from her. People teaching people is often the best method. Scout out persons in your community who have unusual talents or hobbies that are of interest to your group's needs. In most cases, I have found them to be more than willing to come speak, often without remuneration. However, make sure you have communicated with the speakers beforehand, telling them exactly what you can, or cannot, pay. I think it best to give something as an honorarium, even if the guest speaker is coming from your local area. Doing so makes for better community relations!

We had a method in our Sunday school class for paying our invited guests. Refreshments and juices were set up for the brief social time prior to our study session. We did not ask those in attendance to pay, and all first-timers were told they were our guests—but a container for donations was put out each week. We simply reminded those present that it was our method of paying speakers and financing our social activities. Those who could afford to often gave much more than their share; others gave little or nothing. No one was to question those who gave or those who didn't.

Once the members of the class found that I was really interested in their welfare and that of their families, they were supportive of me. When your parishioners feel needed and loved they are more open to growth. Then you can proceed toward a method of integrating them into the total concept of your ministry. To do this you will need a workable procedure.

Establish a Workable Plan

People work much better if they know exactly what it is you expect of them. It is a proven psychological fact that we are all more comfortable in whatever we are doing if we are working with strong leadership. Weak leaders produce weak followers! Individuals coming into our churches and accepting Christ usually pattern their life's attitudes by us. We, the pastors and wives, become their role models.

At this point you may want to go back to your first task of going through your information files to discover any talent that is within the local church body. Once you have done so, the next step will involve organizational policy. While you may never find all the willing workers you need, you can develop new talent. If there is no one available to work on a priority committee of your church, begin a training program. Invite those whom you feel have some ability, or anyone else who might be interested, to work with you in a learning procedure. Don't overlook opportunities afforded your parishioners through high school adult education classes, the local colleges, or the YMCA. All of these provide free, or almost free, training in many areas of learning. Sometimes there are high-schoolers who are eager to help. Just make sure you know what you want and how to accomplish it before asking someone to assist you. Personally, I found it important, as a leader, to ask myself, "What is the priority need of the moment? How can I put this on paper in a way that it can be understood, and how can my directives for accomplishing the task be clearly stated?"

What Is the Priority Need?

EXAMPLE: (Should be written out on file cards for your information only!)

Urgent needs:	Possible persons to do the job:
1. Church bulletin board	Brother Smith, a carpenter
2. Artwork and posters	Sue Smith, an art student

3. Altar arrangement for Mother's Day	Check costs with local florist and ask for sponsors
	See if Jane Downs has the time to do it. Observe the abilities of: Kay Brown Jean Simmons Joy Kilpatrick
4. Persons to be in charge of decor for the upcoming holiday season	

Notes or comments:

After having worked through the initial steps of finding those persons who are interested or willing to learn, you can move on to the next organizational step. You never want to ask Sue Smith to be responsible for the bulletin board without explaining what is expected of her. This can be done through another written form.

Organization and Procedure

EXAMPLE:

Committee: Bulletin board poster display and art

Chairperson:
Sue Smith
243-5867

Duties:
1. Change church bulletin board the first Sunday of each month
2. Create seasonal themes
3. Post all the church's seasonal events

Members:
Desiree Silva
824-3817

Jane Samuels
824-6453

4. Chairperson will clear all outside announcements with the church office or pastor before posting
5. Coordinate any major changes in decor with special activities chairperson
6. Store all unused usable materials in the appointed place
7. Meet once each quarter to coordinate and plan the pro-cedural policy

Budget:
1. Not to exceed $10 monthly
2. Request prerequisite forms through the office one week prior to the need
3. Return all receipts to the church office

NOTE: As a committee member you are not asked to serve on this committee more than twelve months, after which time all personnel will be reassigned.

Signed: _____
Pastor's wife

In case you are wondering why the note at the bottom of the procedure page, there are five reasons for it: 1) No one feels locked into something indefinitely; 2) it elimi-nates having to be strapped with someone who is not cooperative or is not doing a good job; 3) those persons who might like to feel they own a position are less tempted to become possessive of that job; 4) you can integrate new women into the process, as committee members, giving you a chance to observe their work; and 5) new ideas are easier to come by if no one person holds the job longer than a year.

I used the same format for all working committees either in my Sunday school class or in the women's department of the church. Once each year in early spring I arranged for a banquet as formal as our facilities would allow, to have my time of communication with all the women of our church and community. We sometimes brought in a speaker; at other times we didn't. This was known as the "Pastor's Wife's Banquet." All committee members were assigned beforehand and introduced, with appreciation honors being given to those who had served the previous year. At this particular meeting, deacons' wives were seated at the head table, with chairpersons being placed in an honorable position at each of the other tables.

This was always a highlight of our year's work and I tried to make sure of three things: 1) My burden and concern for the ladies was genuine; 2) they understood where the total program was headed; and 3) everything was done ethically, in good taste. All the information was printed out and each woman was given a booklet with names and phone numbers of those working within given areas, so that everyone felt informed. This also helped to eliminate any situation of cliques developing within the church body itself.

In the meantime, during the year, if I wished to make any additions to the committees, or if someone needed to be replaced, I was able to do so. I know it is highly probable you already have your own organizational methods and they may be better than mine! I am also aware that there are some PWs who haven't the slightest idea how to begin. If so, you may take these ideas and modify them to meet your local need. My one suggestion would be that if you are just arriving at a new pastorate, wait a few months before attempting to make major changes in the existing operations of the church. You may not be able to do so even then! A twelve-month waiting period can be a time of incubation for new and creative ideas and working on your own goals and priorities as you get your feet on the ground. You will find it is one thing to have an idea and quite another to get that point across to people with whom you are working.

Going to a church is much like entering into marriage. There are a lot of adjustments on the part of both you and the congregation. No matter how good your intentions may be, if you are to be successful you will need the support of others. Often the persons with whom you will be working must first be convinced of your idea's workability. Once the parishioners have learned to respect you—and it takes time to earn that respect—they will usually give you a great deal of freedom. Don't expect to walk in and have people fall on their faces before you.

After your activities are planned, and your organizational procedures well outlined, you are ready to begin your next step: reaching your community with information about what is happening inside the church. The media can be one of your best outlets for this task.

Take Advantage of Workable Opportunities
Learn something about your local newspaper(s) and use that knowledge to your advantage. You, or someone else, may want to meet with the editor of the special activities section of your paper. If so, go with some well-thought-out questions. Ask, "When is the deadline for weekly articles? What format would you prefer we use? Who is the contact person with whom we can work?" Knowing this will make the editor feel at ease and assist you in doing a better job of communicating.

If your church is small and you have never written a

newspaper article yourself, and have no one in the parish who has, don't be fearful of trying. It is really quite easy to prepare a news release. Some editors with whom I have worked did not want a fully written piece anyway. They preferred the simple information: "what, where, when, who, and how." The form shown below is one I used most recently while giving information to the local church page editor:

SAMPLE:

Name of church:
First Community
2486 Dogwood Road
Anywhere, California

Pastor: Claude H. White
Church office phone:
555-8640
Publicity Chairperson:
Kay Simpkins
Phone: 555-6089

Activity:

WHAT? . . . . Annual Pastor's Wife's Banquet

WHEN? . . . . Tuesday, March 2, at 6:30 P.M.

WHERE? . . . Estes Hall of First Community Church, 2486 Dogwood Road

WHO? . . . . . Speaker will be June Callahan, of Ronsdale, California. June is the area representative for the "Image of Loveliness" organization and will be speaking on the subject "Women and Their Changing Needs." After she has addressed the women on her topic, we will have a time of questions and answers. New committees for the coming year will also be announced at this meeting, and appreciation gifts will be given to those who have worked on church

	committees throughout this past year.
HOW?	There is no cost and all women of the community are invited. For further information and to make reservations, call Joyce Illar at 224-8543 or Ann Miller at 224-9650.

Having done all these things, there is another point to remember: Be consistent in your goals.

Keep Workable Goals before Your People

There will always be a few "sticks in the mud," so don't be discouraged by them. Keep your goals before the people; there will always be those who believe in you and want to help you. There are, of course, other persons who feel they are God's self-appointed ones to see that "things always remain the same." For them, whatever was is always superior to what can be. They live in the past of their ideas and often feel threatened by progress. But when you have established your own credibility as a leader, you may be surprised at how many people will want to follow you. At the close of this chapter, in the Growth Plan section, you will find some ideas to help you get along with those problem people. Always remember that you can't and you won't win all the battles of life, but if you keep on trying and maintain a good attitude you will be a winner regardless of the outcome!

GROWTH PLAN

Dealing with problems
and working with problem people.

1. Isolate any problem areas you might have and don't confuse the issue by feeling everyone is against you.

2. Select what you feel is the best solution to the problem.
3. Develop your plan, your method of operating, and have an alternate plan as well.
4. Recognize the individual rights of others to disagree. Do not take personal affront when they oppose your ideas.
5. Work with the 90 percent who believe in what you are doing and don't get discouraged because of the 10 percent who may not be cooperative.
6. Recognize the complexity of any problem you may have in dealing with people and learn to live with it.
7. Check your own motives; it may well be that a criticism you are getting is legitimate.
8. Give others the same privilege to disagree with you as you take with them.
9. Isolate yourself from the problem, but never from the person; learn what that difference is.
10. Once you have done all you know to do and still do not have the cooperation you need, give the idea more prayerful consideration. This timing might be wrong, or it might be right; either way you will have to be able to take personal responsibility for your actions.

Remember, you are not there to change people but to love them while God does the changing in their lives!

COMMON PERSONALITIES WITH WHICH YOU MUST DEAL

PROFILE	MODE OF BEHAVIOR	POSSIBLE RESPONSE
Ima Quizzer	She will inquire about your welfare, seeking to obtain information.	Give out no information until you know something about the individual (PROV. 18:7).
	"You look troubled—are you all right? Is something wrong with you, your husband, or your family?"	
Paula Possessor	1. Wants to possess every minute of your time. 2. Seeks to be that number one	Don't visit your neighbor too often. You will wear out

116

	woman in your life, the person who has to be in the know of what is going on.	your welcome (PROV. 5:17).
	3. If she doesn't get her way she will often become resentful of you and your friendship toward other women.	
Mabel Merchandiser	1. Endeavors to control you through gifts.	It is better to eat soup with someone you love than steak with someone you hate (PROV. 15:17).
	2. May try to buy her way into your confidence.	
	3. Repeatedly does things for you that could make you feel obligated to her.	
Gerty Gossip	1. Inquisitive about your personal life, how much you paid for what.	Fire goes out for lack of fuel, and tension disappears when gossip stops (PROV. 26:20).
	2. Seeks out information through others.	
	3. Gives out unsolicited information.	
	4. Uses devious methods to find out what she wishes to know.	
	5. Spreads rumors.	
Betty Barter	1. Tells you the intimate secrets of her life, hoping you will tell yours.	If you are looking for advice, stay away from fools (PROV. 14:7).
	2. After having told you all, will turn and ask, "Has this ever happened to you?"	
Guilty Demander	1. Approaches you by asking if you made the call she asked you to make.	Transfer the responsibility back by insisting God has laid the burden upon *her* heart. You will call upon the persons when you can . . . but no promises.
	2. Tries to make you feel guilty by asking, "Will you promise me that you will do it this week?"	

Mary Martyr	1. She tells you she has been sick for a week and no one called on her. 2. Or she has had problems and no one in the church cares, so she's leaving.	Remind her of JAMES 5:14 (KJV), "Is any sick among you? let him call for the elders."
Marge Manipulator	1. Hides behind a facade of shyness to do her dirty deeds of manipulation. 2. She will encourage someone else to say something she doesn't want to be blamed for.	Putting confidence in an unreliable (wo)man is like chewing with a sore tooth (PROV. 25:19).

Suggested Reading:
Jacobs, J. Vernon, *Ten Steps to Leadership,* Standard Press

PART
III

YOU
AND
YOUR
OWN
NEEDS

But sanctify the Lord God in your hearts: and be ready always to give an answer to every man that asketh you a reason of the hope that is in you.
1 PETER 3:15 (KJV).

NINE

Your Spiritual Self

NIBBLING ON GOD'S

WORD MAY CURB

THE SPIRITUAL APPETITE

BUT IT WILL NEVER

SATISFY THE GNAWING

HUNGER FELT BY

THOSE WHO SEEK TO

UNDERSTAND IT.

You can give to others nothing more than what you have!

When the two biblical apostles were en route to a prayer meeting and met the lame man outside the temple gate, they became aware of what they did not have; but they also knew what they *did* have. Seeing the man sitting there in his poverty, one of the disciples looked at him and said, "Silver and gold have I none; but such as I have give I thee" (Acts 3:6, KJV).

What we give to others in spiritual terms is of much more importance than a gift of coins. Our responsibility, especially as PWs, is to give something of eternal value to those we meet. We may not be able to fill the pockets of the poor, or feed all the needy of the world, but we can help those persons around us by giving to them what we have. Before being able to minister to others in a loving and caring way, we must first know what it is to have God touch our own lives. In my book, *Touch Me Again, Lord,*[7] I say:

> *If we are to be effective in touching others we need God's touch. Sometimes it is essential He touch us, not just once but again and again. We then become more and more able to see people with a clearer perspective, and their needs become ours.*

No matter how much our compassionate hearts reach out to people around us, we can never really help them until we have first known God at work in our own lives. *What we have* is what God has bestowed upon us through the free gift of his righteousness. It is out of this resource that we give to others.

How often God has had to remind me of my own limitations! There have been those times when, in my great desire to help others, I myself failed. Somehow, no matter how much I was trying, my efforts were seeming more and more ineffective. When I began to search for the cause it was not too difficult to discover that somewhere in my private devotional life I was guilty of neglect. While seeking to save others, I had allowed my own spiritual welfare to take a second place. That should never have been! Instead of having an ear sharply attuned to the Holy Spirit, I found myself deaf to his tender guidance and unable to hear what those around me were really saying. So, when I reached to take the spiritual cripple by his hand, the handicap in my own life prevented me from being able to hold up the other person. What a disappointment to the one who was hurting, and what an ego-deflating experience for me!

[7]Ruthe White, *Touch Me Again, Lord,* Here's Life

What we try to do in our strengths and with our own abilities fades into insignificance unless it is being done from a heart touched by the fresh presence of the Holy Spirit upon our lives.

Such as we have is what God wants to use. He likes to take that and multiply it for his use. Still we must never forget that spiritual growth and development are not God's responsibility; they are ours. And growth is not an effortless task. God cannot make you a spiritual giant so long as you are content to live on the meager crumbs of his life-giving substance—the Word. You, as a PW, need a working knowledge of the Bible. This does not imply that we are expected to become theologians. It is a simple reminder of the fact that we cannot teach others what we do not know!

As a guest in other clergy homes, I have observed some common characteristics among the more well-adjusted PWs. They have a set time for prayer and Bible study and, while it may be a roughly organized one, they also have a method of study. Each one of them has a place—a desk, kitchen table, or other spot in her home to which she goes for daily devotions. I think such methods are worthy of our consideration.

Setting a Time for Personal Devotions

Setting a time, especially when you have young children, can be difficult. The parsonage schedule makes uninterrupted moments few and far between. My experience has been that the size of the flock matters little. Pressures are largely the same regardless of the number in your congregation. The situation boils down to only one thing: Making time to maintain your spiritual self must become a matter of personal priority. You set the pace of the parsonage, the attitude of your home; and you must never permit the church people to take that from you. In order to maintain consistency in your devotional life, you will have to communicate the reality of that priority to your family, your parishioners, and others.

Whatever method you choose for your quiet time is between you and God. I know women who are such early risers they are able to pull themselves out of bed long before the family awakens. They are then able to have their private moments of prayer and study in relative quietness. There are others of us who are night people. We find it not so easy to make a five o'clock prayer call. I don't believe it is because we love God any less than the early riser does; we just have our inner clocks set to another pace. While I may stagger up before sunrise to take care of household responsibilities, my mind does not catch up with my body until a few hours later. I have learned to solve the problem by doing my work, putting myself together, and setting the timer on the kitchen stove for ten o'clock. When that buzzer goes off, I know it is time for me to put everything else aside and spend a few moments alone with God. There are other times when I have to pray like Ruth Graham, who says she sometimes does it "on the hoof." For years the hour between ten and eleven was my scheduled appointment with God. Now I often find myself on the road, unable to be at my desk and having to work around schedules. I have to do what I can and have a systematic approach to my devotional time. (This doesn't mean I don't talk to God before 10:00 A.M.)

For a long time I hesitated to let my husband's parishioners know my spiritual life habits. (I am a firm believer in entering into your secret closet of prayer without making it a time of fanfare.) But then women would call, asking if they were disturbing me; so I decided to tell them that I was having my personal devotions. This enabled me to call them back without their feeling shut out of my schedule. As years went by, and we were at a church any length of time, we had an unheralded chain of prayer going up in kitchens, clothes closets, and special corners of our homes, as other women joined in with their mid-morning devotions.

Establishing a Place for Study

Every PW needs a little corner, or spot, where she can retreat. You don't need a lot of room, just a place where you can keep your books, a cupful of pencils or pens, your notebook, and those things of importance to you. I have, during my years of church work, used many different areas of the home in which to study. At one parsonage the garage was my private retreat. In another, the kitchen table was my study desk. Once a clothes closet was transformed into a study area. We took the doors off, built shelves onto the wall, dragged in an old desk, and built a study center. For two years now we have been building a home in the San Bernardino, California, mountains. Since we have not yet completed the lower level of our house, the desk occupies one corner of our already-crowded bedroom.

Getting the Equipment You Need

It is not enough to have a place to study; you do need other things as well. You need a table or desk for writing, a reasonably good sitting chair, and some kind of filing system. I started with my files being placed in a cardboard box a little wider than the 12 x 9$^{1/2}$-inch letter folders. There were some manila folders no longer being used at the church, and I was given permission to take them. After changing the old tabs and alphabetizing them according to subject matter, I arranged them in the box. It became a family joke, "Don't mess with Mother's file box!"

In time the material began to grow, and new subjects were added as I clipped ideas from church periodicals, magazines, and newspapers, took notes from speakers, and added my own study notes. The corrugated box was later replaced by a second-hand metal file drawer that grew more and more.

Building Resource Material

Being faithful in study is not enough in itself. You need some method of keeping and retaining what you have learned. We know "the enemy" comes to steal, and that includes anything we may have stored in our subconscious mind. As wonderful and unique as our mental capacities are, they do not always provide us with the instant recall we sometimes need. Of course, we have the promise of God bringing all things to our remembrance (John 14:26), but let us not forget that he does so in many different ways. Sometimes he allows us to run across something, an enlightenment of truth we had long since forgotten; or a minister will stir up our memory; or the Holy Spirit will bring something into our conscious mind. It doesn't really matter what method God uses so long as we are able to grow through it. I feel that filing material is one of the greatest timesavers a PW can have, for these reasons: 1) Once you have written a thought down you have it; 2) if you have it written and filed it is always at your fingertips in a moment's notice; 3) should you wish to study further or pursue a subject, you don't have to start from "scratch" each time. After all, the Apostle Paul spoke about those who were "ever learning, and never able to come to the knowledge of the truth" (2 Tim. 3:7, KJV).

To build your information file you will need to learn to read with a pen and file card in hand. While absorbing a good book on the subject of interest, take advantage of your time by underlining segments and writing down thoughts. If a speaker or author makes a statement that reaches out and grabs you, write it down. I use the procedure as shown here:

SOURCE:	SUBJECT:
Swindoll, Chuck	Discipleship
Improving Your Serve P 48	
Word Books	

Following Christ as his disciple is a costly unselfish decision. It calls for a radical examination of our self-centered life-styles.

When you have finished reading the book, and have written down your ideas, slip the cards into a small metal file box and file them under the letter "D." Now you have ready reference material on the subject of discipleship.

During my personal Bible study time I enjoy writing Scripture in longhand and putting my thoughts on paper. This aids me in the memorization process as I approach the study of God's Word from different angles. This does not mean I play a game of hit-and-miss, or spiritual roulette.

A haphazard study of the Word may be better than nothing, but it is still not good! We all need to adopt some systematic method. Nibbling a bit here and there may curb the spiritual appetite, but it will never satisfy the "gnawing" hunger felt by the person who wants to understand God's Word. It simply will not suffice!

1. The *topical method* is based upon a subject. You trace the topic throughout the Bible by reading cross-references.
2. *Biographical method, or character studies* are profitable in that they provide you with insights into the personalities of those about whom you are reading. Getting to know who wrote what, where the person came from, when the words were written, and to whom, gives much added interest to a biblical context.
3. *Book study* is a method by which one seeks to ascertain the purpose of the writer and his main theme. (It is often helpful to outline a complete book or chapter after having read it.)
4. The *verse-by-verse method* can be an exhaustive word study. A good concordance is helpful in finding other verses that apply toward the same theme. Or, you may want to look up all the words in a verse as they appeared in their original forms.

While seasonal studies are considered topical, they are also an interesting way to build a strong resource file on a particular topic, such as Christmas or Easter. If you study each day of the Passion Week in the life of Christ, read about where he was on each day, and follow the sequence of events leading up to his crucifixion and resurrection, you will appreciate the solemnity of the occasion even more. This year at Christmas I especially enjoyed the season. I ran across some old books hiding in my husband's library that dealt with the Eastern custom of bringing gifts. After having read the books and relating them to the birth of our Lord, I had a much better comprehension of what really occurred on the night of Christ's birth.

If you learn to take full advantage of your reading time by using a file system, you will soon discover that you are being "built up in the most holy faith" through a process of learning. Then, sometime when you get down in spirit (we all have those moments), you can sit at your desk, pick up your notebook, and be encouraged through what you have learned. This is a form of self-encouragement we all need periodically. After all, isn't this what happened to David when he looked out over the ruins of his home, and a city which had been burned by the Amalekites, who had also taken his family captive? The Bible says:

> *And David was greatly distressed; for the people spake of stoning him, because the soul of all the people was grieved, every man for his sons and for his daughters: but David encouraged himself in the Lord his God (1 Sam. 30:6, KJV).*

GROWTH PLAN

Something to help you:
SQR^3 Method of Study

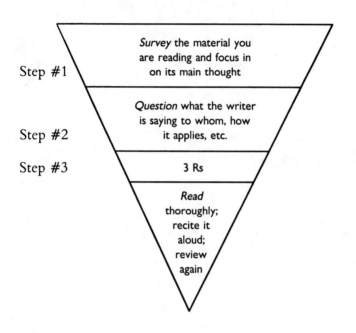

Step #1 — *Survey* the material you are reading and focus in on its main thought

Step #2 — *Question* what the writer is saying to whom, how it applies, etc.

Step #3 — 3 Rs

Read thoroughly; recite it aloud; review again

We learn through repetition and our spiritual growth comes as we develop step by step.

"How beautiful you are, my love, how beautiful!
Your eyes are those of doves. Your hair falls across
your face like flocks of goats that frisk across
the slopes of Gilead. Your teeth are white as sheep's
wool, newly shorn and washed, perfectly matched,
without one missing. Your lips are like a thread of
scarlet—and how beautiful your mouth. Your
cheeks are matched loveliness behind your locks.
Your neck is stately as the tower of David, jeweled
with a thousand heroes' shields."

SONG OF SOLOMON 4:1-4 (TLB)

TEN

Your Physical Self

MOST OF US HAVE BEEN

TAUGHT THAT GOOD

PASTORS' WIVES DON'T

CRY, COMPLAIN, OR

QUESTION THEIR LIFE'S

WORK, THEY SIMPLY

ACCEPT IT.

Accepting your physical limits can be an invaluable step toward personal growth. In order to come to this point you will have to learn how to recognize the signals your body is giving out. Most of us, as PWs, have difficulty in determining what those signals are. You may be no different than the rest of us!

We don't like to accept the fact that our bodies take on a negative response when exposed to continued stress, emotional upheavals, and physical exhaustion. We act as if these things could be happening to everyone else, but never to us. There may even be some PWs among us who have not been trained to handle their emotions and the anger they sometimes feel. I suspect that most of us have been taught that good PWs don't cry, complain, or question their life's work . . . they simply accept it.

This is certainly true in my own case. Since I was raised by parents who had lived through the Depression years, I grew up with the work ethic being understood. No member of our family was permitted to stop working until all chores were done. When Claude and I entered into full-time ministry, I carried the same philosophical approach right into the parsonage. Only I was soon to discover that my work was never done! You will find, as I did, that in church ministry there's always more to be accomplished, new goals to reach, unfinished tasks waiting to be completed, and plenty of people who are willing to praise you for what you are doing, while they sit back and let you carry the burden of responsibility. Unfortunately for me, I had no mentor who could give me guidance in my role. It was several years into our pastoral work, after five years of chronic infection, that a medical doctor asked me the proverbial $64,000 question, "Ruthe, do you expect to get a greater reward when you get to heaven because you died young?"

A dear Black friend, whose husband pastored a neighboring Baptist church in our city, gave me a humorous but startling revelation of what life was all about. It was during my aforementioned health problems that Sister Williams (that's what her husband's parishioners called her) sat visiting with me in my living room. She knew I was scheduled for surgery the following day. Of course, the parsonage phone was ringing and I was answering it. When people inquired as to how I was feeling, my usual reply was, "I am fine!" I had no sooner put the phone back onto the hook, after an extensive conversation with someone, when Mrs. Williams pulled her chair up beside mine.

Without blinking, she looked squarely into my face and said: "You lie, you lie to those church people and you are going to die. When you do those folk at the church are going to gather 'round you and cry and cry. They will say,

134

'She sure was a good woman and worked hard'; then those women are going to start in fussin' over which one gets your man!"

She didn't know it, but she was giving me a great motivation to keep on living. (Maybe she *did* know!) One thing was for sure: I wasn't ready to relinquish my wifely rights, not yet.

You may be asking yourself: *But where do I draw the line and how do I know when enough is enough?* You can, and must, begin to watch for the caution lights and slow up at the intersections of new responsibility. Before saying "yes" to another project, think it over first, pray about it, seek to know if God is really directing you in the step.

We know that every major highway in this vast network of roads in the U.S. has both "stop" and "go" signs. In between the red and green is a yellow caution. We would do well, as PWs, to recognize the flashing of our inner warning systems. The yellow light is blinking when we get migraine headaches, nervous twitches, painful menstrual symptoms, insomnia, and other unexplainable pains. These are signs meant to slow us down. We would do well to respect the electronic mechanism that is signaling us to a STOP! Note, there is a difference between stopping temporarily and quitting.

STOP!
1. When you feel yourself becoming resentful of your role.
2. When your husband, children, or any one person becomes the target of your anger, even if that anger is unexpressed.
3. When you feel one particular person is your enemy and is *the one* who has set out to get you.
4. When you feel "boxed in" by all the pressures coming toward you.
5. When you find yourself crying out, "God, where are you?"

6. When you have recurring anxiety and are living under the dread of some unexplainable fear.
7. When your body begins to react with repeated attacks of asthma, allergies, PMS, migraines, or other pains the doctor cannot diagnose.
8. When you feel God is angry, or is being unfair with you.
9. When your family indicates you are neglecting them and their needs.
10. When you have been involved in an extensive project that has stretched over weeks or months.

There are other times too when you may need a brief pause from your daily work schedule. Maybe it's just a short breathing space of one day. Communicate your needs to your family, explain to them why you feel as you do, that you need a place and time to recoup.

It may mean only a few hours that you mark off your calendar and do something for yourself. You might want to give yourself a much-needed perm, shape your nails, or do something else just for yourself.

As Christians we tend to put great emphasis on the intrinsic, spiritual part of our lives. Rightly so! But sometimes we internalize all our efforts without taking time to care for the outer temple as well. PWs are especially vulnerable, to the point of neglecting their own needs while helping others.

Protect What God Has Given You
Protecting yourself means caring for your body's needs, eating properly, taking vitamins, getting a reasonable amount of sleep, and doing those things necessary for the maintenance of good health. After all, is it not good common sense that we will produce more when we are feeling well? To have a positive self-concept we need to care for, and about, our physical appearance. We *can* do so without going overboard in diet-

ing, exercise, clothes, or makeup. It is not carnal pride to want to look and feel well!

You don't have to have a lot of money to look fashionable. Most PWs are geniuses at knowing how to keep their wardrobes in top-notch shape on a small budget. And you can be well dressed if you own only one good outfit. The secret is not in how much you spend, but how you spend it! By purchasing only one new suit a year you can look as "spiffy" as you need to—that is, provided you buy wisely and give your clothes proper care. You may be sitting there wishing you could afford one outfit a year. I can understand your predicament. While my husband was in training and early ministry, I found myself going for years without being able to replace my one good outfit. During that time I changed the collar, added velvet lapels, made myself some contrasting neck scarves, replaced the suit's zipper, and kept right on wearing it. Since then I have been introduced to the wonders of sales and credit card shopping.

When moving to a new city, one of my first business moves is to make application for a credit card. I like to apply at one of the better department stores because they seem to have the best sales. The two times each year that I use the plastic money are after Christmas and in late summer, when I hit the clearances. Because I carry the store's credit card I am informed when their best sales are coming up. I feel my money is worth more if it is invested in a garment that is worth twice what I pay (than if I paid the same price for two poorly made outfits without style). If you have an aversion to any credit card buying at all, that is certainly your prerogative. I have discovered, in my case, that often an emergency will arise and I am without a basic pair of shoes, or something I must have. When this occurs it usually means I have to pay full price for an article of lesser quality, or shoes that are too wide for my feet. In any instance, whether by cash or credit, we know discretion is a must, and something is not always a bargain just because it's on sale.

Before taking the plunge of buying the one suit you know you will be wearing for years, ask yourself:

1. What else do I have in my wardrobe with which this will coordinate? (Most fashion experts feel you should have at least three: skirts, blouses, or jackets.)
2. How long has this style been around? (If you have seen it being worn for the last four seasons you know it will be outdated in about another year, unless it is a classic.)
3. Is the color one that is best for me? Is it a faddish shade that will become obsolete within the next five years?
4. How are the inner seams of the garment finished? What is the quality of the fabric—does it wrinkle, is it serviceable to my needs, is it washable?
5. What shoes do I have that can be worn with the suit?

You can update an old suit by using new accessories. Take your old blouses, cut off the sleeves about elbow length. Run an inch hem in them, and wear the blouses with your summer skirts. (You can give your husband's long sleeve dress shirts the same treatment.) Replace your old blouse with one having the newer lines and the look of the season.

If you don't have a transitional wrap, or a light evening one, you might want to do what I did. Purchase one yard of fifty-eight-to-sixty-inch-wide woolen fabric. Lay the material flat and fold it on a bias. Cut through the center bias fold, making two triangular pieces of fabric. Fringe the two outer edges by pulling threads from one end to the other until you have made a fringe border about three inches long. Then zigzag stitch along the upper part of the fringe and hem the piece across the bias cut. This makes a wonderful traveling wrap and provides you with a high fashion look at a low cost.

When buying shoes (preferably black, brown, tan, or beige) try to get them on sale. Stay away from white shoes unless you are very thin. White makes a woman's ankles

Pattern for Shoulder Wrap

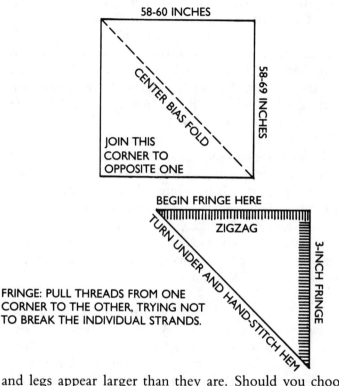

58-60 INCHES

58-69 INCHES

CENTER BIAS FOLD

JOIN THIS
CORNER TO
OPPOSITE ONE

BEGIN FRINGE HERE

ZIGZAG

TURN UNDER AND HAND-STITCH HEM

3-INCH FRINGE

FRINGE: PULL THREADS FROM ONE
CORNER TO THE OTHER, TRYING NOT
TO BREAK THE INDIVIDUAL STRANDS.

and legs appear larger than they are. Should you choose to purchase white, don't invest a lot of money. Plan to dye the shoes in late summer. I have found that the large felt, permanent magic markers do a superb job of dying synthetic and leather strap sandals. Just make sure to use the kind of marker that doesn't wash off when the shoes come in contact with water.

Give Your Skin and Hair Proper Care

You don't have to buy expensive creams to take proper care of your complexion. Some skin experts have said that by neglecting to properly cleanse the face just one night before going to bed, we add an extra seventy-two hours of aging to our skin. Most recently, an entire television program was dedicated to this topic, and women were encouraged to use facial products found in their homes. One example was given of a movie star who is said to use nothing on her face for cleansing except Crisco vegetable shortening. During the leaner years of our ministry I used facial concoctions my mother taught me to make while on the farm. Later on in life, I adapted other ingredients to meet my own specific needs. (Some of the recipes are included in the growth section of this chapter.)

You can improve your self-image by getting a well-shaped haircut. You may not feel you can afford a weekly set, and that isn't necessary. By going to your beautician (or someone else who can cut your hair) at intervals of four to six weeks, you can keep your hair in good shape. In most cases it is the cut that makes the difference in manageability.

Now, just in case you are one of those women who feels this to be an exercise in vanity, read the account of the woman in Song of Solomon:

> *"Kiss me again and again, for your love is sweeter than wine. How fragrant your cologne. . . . My darling bride is like a private garden, a spring that no one else can have, a fountain of my own. You are like a lovely orchard bearing precious fruit, with the rarest of perfumes; nard and saffron, calamus and cinnamon, and perfume from every other incense tree" (Song of Sol. 1:1; 4:12-14, TLB).*

GROWTH PLAN

Oatmeal Facial Scrub:
Put two tablespoons of oatmeal in a blender and process until it is like coarse flour. Mix with two teaspoons of cornmeal. Apply by adding water and rubbing into your face in a circular, upward motion. Rinse well and moisturize.

1/2 tsp. honey
1/2 tsp. white vinegar
1 tbsp. spirit of camphor
1 cup rosewater
Drops of perfume (optional)

Facelift:
One cup fresh buttermilk
1 tsp. dry skim milk
1 tsp. spirit of camphor
1 tsp. mint extract

Whip together, apply to face, throat, and neck and allow to dry for about 10–15 minutes.

Bath Oil:
1 cup shampoo
1 pint baby oil or safflower or vegetable oil

Resource Aids:
Barnes, Emilie, *More Hours in My Day,* Harvest House
Luckey, Camilla, *You Can Live on Half Your Income,* Zondervan
Nethery, Betty and Smith, Beverly B., *Uniquely You,* Tyndale

Note: Manning Dress Outlets have agreed to give an added 10 percent to all ministers' wives who refer to this book, giving my name as reference.

Manning Silver Dress Outlets:

1150 Santee (between 11th & 12th Los Angeles St. & Maple)
Los Angeles, Cal.
(213) 749-8339

9067 Venice Blvd. (2 blocks west of Robertson on north side of street.)
Culver City, Cal.

The man who sets a trap for others will get caught in it himself. Roll a boulder down on someone, and it will roll back and crush you.
PROVERBS 26:27 (TLB)

ELEVEN

Your Ethics

ETHICS IS THE UNDER-

LYING VALUE SYSTEM

UPON WHICH YOUR

LIFE'S DECISIONS

ARE BASED.

You can't learn ethics simply by reading a textbook! According to Webster's dictionary, ethics is a set of principles that deals with your behavioral responses toward your peers. It is the underlying value system upon which your life is based. Knowing a code of ethics may be helpful to you in broadening your understanding of what others expect in a given situation; it does not guarantee them you will respond accordingly. You are the one who makes the decision as to whether you will or will not act within a given standard of conduct.

Webster
Latin: Ethical—conforming to a professional standard of conduct.

Each profession has its written or or unwritten rules of expected professional behavior. Those working within that vocation are judged by their peers and encouraged to live within the norms decided upon.

We, as PWs, also have an obligation to work according to guidelines considered ethical in the ministerial profession. While it may be true that our roles have never been clearly defined, and no church denomination (at least to my knowledge) has set down any clear-cut dos and don'ts for the clergy, we are not exempt from the Golden Rule, "Do unto others as we would have others do unto us." Living by this principle is not always easy, not even in the parsonage. Perhaps this is the reason all three of the apostles—Matthew, Mark, and Luke—recorded these words of Jesus:

> *"If anyone wants to be a follower of mine, let him deny himself and take up his cross and follow me. For anyone who keeps his life for himself shall lose it; and anyone who loses his life for me shall find it again" (Matt. 16:24, 25; see Mark 8:34; Luke 9:23, TLB).*

To take up your cross and follow Christ may mean you will have to risk being misunderstood by those you love, and who love you! Every pastor and wife have been or will be called upon, to act in such a manner as to bring about a breach in ministerial relationships. We are often "pitted," one against the other, by friends and well-meaning people. Because of this it is important for us to remember that it is our responsibility to take the initiative in the matter. We may have to sacrifice some of our pride and ego in order to do this. Parishioners are, in most cases, unaware of ministerial codes of ethics. Because of this they sometimes ask us to participate in activities that might be offensive, or not fully understood by another pastor or PW.

Example: Former members call, asking if our husband will return to a city where he once pastored to perform a wedding. This can be a really sticky situation. We must be careful at this point that we do not let our emotions enter into our decision. As a PW it is best to set no dates and confirm no appointments in relation to these requests until we have gone through the proper channels. Most church leaders with whom I have discussed this topic insist that protocol dictates the policy: 1) The former member should be referred back to the present pastor of the church; 2) the invitation for your coming should be initiated through the existing pastor; 3) all plans for the wedding would be communicated through the pastor to you. While you may be running the risk of being misunderstood by those calling you, you are also acting in good faith toward the minister who now serves them. It is always good to remind these parishioners that your husband is no longer their pastor. To infringe upon their present pastor's ministry and enter his sphere of influence without his invitation would be highly unethical.

Why Be Ethical?

Those outside the church often judge the whole of the Christian community as they observe our ethics. This is especially true when it comes to our financial dealings. In an earlier chapter I mentioned the need for sometimes using a credit card. One sure way to bring havoc to the kingdom of God is in the area of special treatment. Unfortunately, a few ministerial families have made it difficult for the rest of us. There have been times when I have walked into business establishments ashamed to reveal my husband's profession, because of the testimony some other minister had left. Many times we have been told that ministers are hard to deal with, that they expect too many favors and won't pay their bills. I know this is not the norm. Those persons in the ministry with whom we have had contact are, on the whole, honest and conscientious men and women.

For a minister and family to live on the brink of bankruptcy is one of the most devastating reproaches that could come to our profession. Living to the "hilt" on your salary can be a temptation to any PW. If you feel you must have things to be happy, make sure you do not have them at the expense of your husband's ministry. I know how difficult it is to live on a budget when your income is low. But to spend beyond your ability to pay is morally and ethically wrong. According to authorities on the matter of credit, we are told that eligibility for a loan is based upon the three Cs: 1) Character and your willingness to repay the debt; 2) capacity to pay; and 3) capital that enables you to pay. To borrow money under false pretense is to bring a reproach on the ethical conduct of your profession.

Another reason for being ethical is to challenge others to do the same; and you will never be at your best more than when you, by your actions, encourage others to live on the highest level of their better selves. People have a tendency to become what you encourage them to be. You remember the story of how Mordecai, in his great concern for the safety of the Jewish people, risked his own life in making an appearance before King Ahasuerus wearing his mourning garments of sackcloth and ashes. When Queen Esther, whom most commentators believe to have been Mordecai's cousin, saw what was happening, she inquired as to the cause of his actions. Having then been informed of Haman's plan to destroy all of the Jews, the Queen was faced with a decision. Mordecai's great concern for his people prompted the challenge to Esther. He, by risking his life to do the right thing, was presenting his young cousin with a similar choice of action. The man must have felt rewarded when his relative rose to the heights of her inner self and declared, "And so will I go in unto the king, which is not according to the law: and if I perish, I perish (Esther 4:16b, KJV).

How Do You Apply Ethics?
To apply methods of ethical behavior means you will have to recognize the rights of others. One older pastor addressed a group of younger ministers and said: "Make sure your love for people is just one degree behind your love for God. You can never help people without loving them. By people I mean not just the lovely, but the unlovely as well. The

quickest way to curtail your effectiveness is by isolating yourself with just a few friends. Your heart must be like a harbor ready to receive ships from many lands."

It is often tempting for us to feel that our obligations, as PWs, do not extend to the troublemaker or the disgruntled. What we often fail to consider is that others may see us in somewhat the same manner in which we perceive them.

My husband tells the story of his having prayed that God would relieve him of a woman in the church who was a troublemaker. His only way out seemed to be to ask God to call her home. He laughingly confessed his longing to conduct her funeral. But when he found himself praying about it, God seemed to have a different idea. He said, "God spoke to my heart and told me, 'I don't want her either.'" Of course, this was not really a true incident. It does, however, illustrate our selfish motives in wanting God to remove those people who are often in greatest need of our help. When he allows them to be there, God is also asking us to give them their rights, and the same privileges we take!

Being ethical involves the little things in life too! It means that you will earnestly seek to smooth the path of life, making it easier for another PW to follow you. One thing is for sure, if you cannot lighten another person's load you do not have to make his burden heavier. This was made increasingly clear to me, as a young pastor's wife, when we followed an older ministerial family in a pastorate.

V. L. and Erma Hertweck had lived in their community for about five years. They were greatly loved by those inside and outside the church. When they decided to make a move, they chose to recommend that the church board interview us. My husband was elected as the new pastor. It was when we were moving into the parsonage that I came to realize just how much another PW can do to make another's path smoother.

The movers had just begun to unload our meager furniture when I saw a notebook resting on the kitchen cabinet beside the telephone. In the spiral binder was a series of handwritten notes telling me where to find what in our new city. Erma had given me the names and phone numbers of doctors, hairdressers, preferred cleaning establishments, and told me how to find the best of everything. There was a committee report showing me how the women's department of the church was organized, and which woman served in what capacity. Information was given as to who was in the hospital and needed immediate attention. Food was prepared and sitting on the kitchen table. The parsonage was left sparkling clean.

My husband invited the Hertwecks back to the church just as quickly as our schedule permitted their coming. Still, during the six years we pastored there, though they were our pulpit guests many times, never did they come into our city without first calling us. We were informed as to their expected arrival and departure. While visiting they were most cautious about accepting dinner dates without being sure we were invited. Sometimes we chose to go; other times we didn't, depending upon our schedule of activities. We invited both of them to return anytime they wished, knowing our position would always be strengthened by their coming.

On the other hand, I have had other PWs speak with me about the disappointment they felt when a former pastor and wife spent vacations with parishioners, stayed as guests in their homes, and socialized with them, without having given the present pastor and family the courtesy of telling them they were in town. A pastor's wife talked with me about how difficult it was in one pastorate because a former minister's wife kept in such close telephone contact with the church ladies that she could never get them to organize things her own way. It seems the PW who preceded her was dictating policies long after her husband had left the church.

Another PW shared her feelings of hurt as she spoke of

the attitude of a former pastor regarding the new carpet that was being installed. Seeing the remains of the old carpet cast aside in a heap and soon to be carted away to the dump was too much for the man to handle. The former pastor voiced his feelings openly to those members working on the project by saying: "How could they do this to my carpet? I had this put in years ago. Just think how many prayers have been prayed and tears shed on this rug." Needless to say, before Sunday came, the woman knew they were in trouble. She felt the aftermath of his remarks when she arrived for worship. There was such a division over the new carpet that it caused a problem for them later. Some of the members wanted progress, to see some changes made, while others agreed with the former pastor.

We all know there are some problems we can't avoid! Even so, you and I can leave a pastorate with dignity. When we feel we have been the victims of unthoughtful and vicious people we still have an obligation to withdraw gracefully. (This is not to say we don't feel, sometimes respond with negative thoughts, and wish we could do something.) It means that we pray for good to come out of the situation, seek to act according to biblical principles, and commit to God those things we can do nothing about. Even if we are mad at the deacons, and feel rejected by the church, we dare not take vengeance into our own hands. We may win the battle but lose the war. When we choose to do what is right before God, seeking the growth of his kingdom, we can walk away with our heads held high.

Ethics Reveal Our General Attitudes Toward Others

Being ethical may mean you will have to go the second mile in dealing with people. Building good relationships means that someone has to bend, going beyond the call of duty to keep harmony among people and on a staff. One senior PW friend shared with me her philosophy in working with younger members—wives of men on staff—by keeping in close touch with what has happening to them. She said they met each month, talked about how they felt, where they were hurting, and how they could help each other.

Another PW invited me to be her guest at a luncheon meeting of the women on pastoral staff. We met at a lovely restaurant at a time prearranged by the senior pastor's wife. After finishing the meal they took up the agenda of the day. There was some discussion of how to handle the gift giving in their church. The congregation had grown from around 500 to near 2,000. This meant they would need to set some policy as to what they should give to brides, at baby showers, and as general gifts. They discussed the feasibility of one present from the office staff, a standard item or something of equal value that would be decided upon. After they had discussed the pros and cons they agreed to approach it by giving a cup and saucer in the pattern of the bride's china, and an engraved New Testament for all new babies born to church members. They were to see that not one member of the group broke rank to do something "special" for a particular person. One thing was evident—everyone was to be treated equally!

There are other ways too in which our attitude shows. People are always measuring our values by the manner in which we respond to what they do for us. No one likes, respects, or wants to be around a PW who is an ingrate. It takes so little time and energy to call someone and say "thanks" for the covered dish or other thoughtful gift. I have observed that those PWs who are prompt in sending thank-you notes and show their sincere gratitude are genuinely thoughtful people. They have trained themselves to respond to the efforts of others in a meaningful way.

There are little ways in which you can learn to become more thoughtful in your daily responsibilities. You can:

1. Be prompt in sending notes of appreciation. If possible, send them within two weeks of the occasion.
2. You can arrive as a guest for a dinner engagement on

time. This means no earlier than ten minutes when eating in someone's home and no later than ten minutes after.

3. If you are more than ten minutes late, you should call and tell the hostess what time she can expect you.

4. If it is a dinner party you have been invited to attend and you are detained because of an emergency, the hostess should be told to go ahead with the meal.

5. After you arrive, begin eating at whatever course is being served at the time. Don't expect your hostess to reheat your meal and leave her other guests sitting alone.

6. Make sure, if you have to cancel an appointment, that it is done well in advance. Don't let the other party down at the last minute.

7. Use the post office as a liaison of goodwill. Send notes of appreciation to your ladies who have done a good job serving on a committee. You may feel someone is hurting, needs your special attention, and would appreciate a note from you during the week. To perform this courtesy may mean less time spent in a counseling session later on.

8. Make all appointments from your calendar and don't depend upon your memory.

9. When invited out while at church or a gathering, tell the party you will get back with her, then don't forget to follow up.

10. Keep a calendar of events. I think it best if you do not carry it to the church meetings (other than planning sessions). Reason: People will try to set up dates while looking over your shoulder. When you tell them you are busy they often point to some unmarked date and ask, "How about this?"

(Other suggestions are included in the growth plan that may prove helpful to you also.)

One of the most difficult aspects of dealing with this

subject is knowing that what may be totally acceptable in one denomination may be considered unethical in another. So, for that reason, we cannot set an ironclad code of conduct and expect everyone to live by it. Still there is one tool of measurement by which every PW should seek to live: "Do as we would have others do unto us."

GROWTH PLAN

Some things to consider:

1. Don't insist on staying on at a church after the senior pastor has left without first clearing it with your denominational officials.
2. Don't get caught in the "buffer zone" between your husband and the people. If they have anything to say to him, let them go directly to him.
3. Don't share your personal life with members of the parish.
4. Don't bring criticism upon yourself, or your family, by being seen in a public place with someone of the opposite sex without a third party in attendance.
5. Don't call speakers and then automatically assume that you can tape their speech or message. It may be that they have their own professional tapes and want to keep some control over what is being sold. In most cases, if they do they will work out a selling arrangement with you.
6. Don't use other people's material without giving them credit.
7. Don't mimeograph pages from periodicals or make duplicate tapes without first getting permission from the person who has first rights.
8. Don't expect more of someone else than you would do. If you call a speaker, provide adequate housing in a safe and comfortable surrounding.

9. Don't permit a wife of a guest speaker to sit alone in the sanctuary. Meet her upon arrival and invite her to sit with you.
10. Don't let a visiting minister and wife leave your church without your making their acquaintance.

"*If you welcome a prophet because he is a man of God, you will be given the same reward a prophet gets. And if you welcome good and godly men because of their godliness, you will be given a reward like theirs.*"

MATTHEW 10:41 (TLB)

TWELVE

Your Hospitality

HOSPITALITY IS NEITHER FORMAL ENTERTAINING NOR AN INFORMAL GATHERING. IT IS A BIT OF BOTH: THE IMPROMPTU AND THE PLANNED TIMES OF SHARING, WHEN WE GIVE TO OTHERS WHAT WE HAVE AND ALLOW THEM TO SHARE A PART OF THEM- SELVES WITH US.

Hospitality is twofold: It causes us to make room for other people in our lives, giving them the opportunity to share what they have with us, and we with them.

One of the first biblical examples of this is found in Genesis as Abraham entertained three men who came to him on the Plains of Mamre.

> *This is the way it happened: One hot summer afternoon as he was sitting in the opening of his tent, he suddenly noticed three men coming toward him. He sprang up and ran to meet them and welcomed them.*
>
> *"Sirs," he said, "please don't go any further. Stop awhile and rest here in the shade of this tree while I get water to refresh your feet, and a bite to eat to strengthen you. Do stay awhile before continuing your journey."*
>
> *"All right," they said, "do as you have said."*
>
> *Then Abraham ran back to the tent and said to Sarah, "Quick! Mix up some pancakes! Use your best flour, and make enough for the three of them!" (Gen. 18:1-6, TLB).*

Throughout both the Old and New Testaments we are given numerous examples of those who provided food and lodging for weary travelers. Jesus, in his day, was often blessed by those who extended their hospitality toward him. Do you remember the occasion when Zacchaeus, the short man in the tall tree, invited the Lord to eat with him? Zacchaeus' invitation was an impromptu one, not premeditated or planned. It was an action of the heart, one Jesus recognized and accepted.

We also know that Jesus was a frequent guest in the home of Martha, Mary, and Lazarus. Their Bethany residence was a place the Lord visited most often. When we look at the strongly independent natures of the persons living there, and sense the love they shared, we can understand why Jesus enjoyed their friendship so much.

Martha was, beyond doubt, the gourmet cook of her day. She could prepare Jewish cuisine that would satisfy the palate of her most fastidious guest. She was a perfectionist right down to the last detail of entertainment etiquette. Martha always checked to see that her formal tablecloth measured a precise eighteen inches from the table's edge. (Emily Post says a formal dinner cloth should measure eighteen inches from the table's edge. A buffet cloth may reach the floor if one desires.) Martha's culinary delights were served with a flourish: a sprig of mint or parsley always rested on top of her roasted, curried lamb. (Now don't criticize Martha for this. The words of our Lord to her dealt more with attitude than with her meticulousness.)

Mary, the other sister, was a different kind of person. I believe her to have been the mood-setter. It was she who picked the lilies of the field and arranged them in the alabaster vase, placing them at the head of the table where Jesus reclined while eating.

She was also the philosophical one of the three. Mary loved going to the synagogue, listening to the scribes reading from the Scroll, and reveling in the arguments that were ongoing between the scribes and Pharisees. Had Mary been living in our day she would have been the family member who bought the FM stereo. Beethoven, Bach, and Chopin would have been among Mary's favorite composers. We don't have to stretch our imaginations too far to visualize her, sitting at the feet of Jesus, weighing every word he is saying, trying to grasp the hidden meanings of his illustrations, absorbing every word.

Then, there was their brother Lazarus, the businessman of Bethany. When he walked down the street people knew him, called him by name, and respected him. He was the kind of person to whom Jesus could speak man to man. The two of them trusted each other and could talk freely of the political issues of their day. They may have discussed the Law, and the purpose of the temple in Jerusalem, as Lazarus inquired of its future. He might have queried Jesus regarding the overthrow of the Roman yoke, as he chafed beneath its bondage. We know the two men had a strong friendship, because it was at the tomb of Lazarus that Jesus wept. Then, after his friend had been dead for five days, our Lord called him forth—by name!

Think with me: *If they had never opened their Bethany home in hospitality, would they have known the life-giving resurrection power of the Messiah?*

We miss so much blessing, both for ourselves and for others, by failing to obey the biblical command to "share with God's people who are in need. Practice hospitality" (Rom. 12:13, NIV).

The writer to the Hebrews warned us to be careful lest we entertained angels unaware (Heb. 13:2). It was this injunction that caused our youngest daughter some problems. Her father had excused himself from the table to answer the door. His standing there in a long conversation with the man who had rung the doorbell, while the rest of us continued eating, was confusing to her barely-five-year-old mind. She proceeded to ask a few questions regarding the matter: "Mommy, what's that man doing coming to our house? Why do people come over when we are eating our dinner?"

"Well, honey," I said to her, "the Bible tells us to be kind to strangers because they might be God's angels . . . angels unaware."

Looking up at me, unable to interpret my words, she replied in her own impish manner:

"Yeah, Mom, they probably are angels in underwear, all right!"

That ended our lesson in hospitality for the day.

Hospitality Is More Than a Formality

Hospitality in its earliest concept was a sevenfold one (Judges 19:20-23).

1. Receiving of guests and imparting a salutation of peace and blessing upon them.
2. Sharing of personal supplies.

3. Providing lodging.
4. Bringing guests into one's home and sharing in a congenial manner (v. 20).
5. Giving food to guests' animals or beasts of burden (v. 21).
6. Washing of feet or furnishing a basin of water for their cleansing (v. 21; Luke 7:36-50).
7. Preparing food and setting it before the guest.

Hospitality is simply the sharing of what one has. *After all, God never requires of us more than we have to give!* One of the excuses used most frequently by PWs is, "I am afraid that what I have will not be good enough for them." That statement is nothing more than an excuse.

My husband is a man who likes to have his friends come over. It doesn't really matter to him whether I am serving a formal dinner or something simple, if he chooses to invite them as guests. In the earlier stages of our ministry there were days when I never knew for how many I might be cooking at night. On one occasion he had gone golfing with several of his buddies. After they had finished the game, he called me, saying he might bring one of the men home with him for dinner. Since that meant only one extra serving, I agreed. It was one of those foggy days we sometimes have in Southern California—a perfect time for me to drag out the old Sears sewing machine. I was enjoying the "buzz" of each stitch as the needle went up and down, welding the seams of my dress together. The chili beans I had put on early that morning were bubbling away in the crockpot as the spicy herbs filtered through the house and into the room where I was working. Dinner for us that day was going to be southern style—chili and cornbread. I had just enough cornmeal for the bread, and only one egg. Having reasoned in my mind that it would be plenty for my family plus one, I was all set for a day's sewing.

When Claude arrived home I was shocked to discover he had brougnt along both the man *and* his wife. I had known her only by passing acquaintance and she had never been in our home before. There was *no* way I could avoid registering my surprise as she entered the house. It was much too late for me to do anything other than serve what I had already planned to feed my family. The beans were plentiful but the cornbread was a bit skimpy. The house still looked like a sewing center, with the machine out, material and patterns scattered over the bed, and the ironing board not yet put away.

I have not, to this day some twelve years later, apologized to my friend about the incident. However, that pastor's wife and I have become wonderful pals. (I must tell you, though, that Claude caught it for not communicating with me a little better.)

Another time, right after we were married, while living in temporary housing and waiting to move into the church-owned youth parsonage, Claude decided to bring the bishop of our denomination home for dinner. You will understand my feelings of lost pride when I tell you there was no inside plumbing in our two-room student housing project apartment. In a corner of the small room that doubled for a clothes closet and kitchen we had an apartment-sized stove and a breakfast table. Besides those limitations, I was a new-bride cook.

The bishop came and seemed to enjoy what we had to offer. I had no matching silver or china. What I could give was hospitality, food served on a freshly starched tablecloth in a clean and pleasant environment. From that day forward the bishop never forgot the young couple from California who had opened their hearts to him.

Missionaries were always welcome in our domain. I liked having them come because they added so much to our children's lives. Each missionary who stayed in our home was asked to autograph the flyleaf of the girls' Bibles. They would often write short notes, or sign their names in the native language of the country from which they worked.

(Don't misunderstand me on this: I am a firm believer in respecting the privacy of the home and family. You can have too many people coming through your doors. But what seems to be missing in our society is the joy of opening our homes and sharing our daily fare, as opposed to taking our guests out to eat.) The thought of having someone stay at your house may conjure up visions of polishing silver, washing china, and serving nine-course dinners. No; that is *entertaining!* To serve what you have in a less formal way is hospitality.

Having people in at the last moment, or inviting a group to come over for an impromptu time of fun, can be exciting. Consider soup dinners, fondue parties, waffle breakfasts, barbecues, salad luncheons, or pizza parties. Try using other foods that can be prepared ahead of time, or whipped up on a moment's notice. One pastor's wife says she is never caught without an extra package of spaghetti and a jar of sauce. She knows that by adding a quick salad she can always stretch it into a meal. I am told Vonette Bright of Campus Crusade always keeps frozen or canned chicken on hand. She can make a quick lunch by tossing the chicken with a green salad. For an elegant evening meal the chicken can be used with a cream sauce over frozen/baked pastry shells.

In our area there is a group of about six ministers and their wives who enjoy getting together every few months. We meet at the various homes and stick pretty much to one format. Monday is our usual meeting day, with arrival time after 4:00 P.M. Couples bring their own meat to barbecue; prearranged fruit or vegetable salad plates are brought; and the hostess furnishes the drinks. We start to barbecue around 5:00, then serve the food, keeping the procedure as simple as possible. When the meal is finished we spend the evening sharing, and sometimes just having fun, playing games, and laughing together. This time is valuable to each one of us as we forget our "roles" and accept each other's friendship. This provides all of us with the opportunity of being ourselves and knowing the others understand our feelings.

Hospitality is genuine thoughtfulness toward others. It must come from your heart, expressing a part of your personality; otherwise you will only be acting out an expected form of behavior. If this is a problem for you, ask God to help you in this area of your life. While dealing with ethics in the preceding chapter, I talked about some things we could do to make others feel more comfortable in our church surroundings. The same rule applies to both our homes and the church. If you are entertaining a speaker or friend in your home over a period of days, allow the person as much privacy as possible. Provide a comfortable chair, something he can write on, and pencil and paper close at hand. A bowl of fruit and a single rosebud in a vase are some of the little touches you can add. If your home is crowded, as many parsonages are, show the guest how to find extra linens and give him a brief rundown as to your schedule. He will appreciate knowing what time the children leave for school, when the facilities are available, and what time you plan to eat the evening meal.

If you are the guest, respect the privacy of that home; eat what is served; be there when the family plans the meals; stay out of the way when the children are getting off in the mornings; and make your own bed. Pick up after yourself and assist the hostess as much as you, and she, are comfortable with.

Having people drop by during the holidays is always fun for me. One PW friend I know sometimes has an open house during the Christmas season. She decorates their home in early December and sets aside one weekend from Friday through Sunday for the open house. She divides the church family up alphabetically, allowing two-hour segments for each group. She and her husband serve punch and cookies. Pastries are brought in on plates by the individual families, who share with them during that time.

(This plan may work better in a smaller church setting.)

Informality has its place, and there are times when it is more acceptable than formal entertainment. However, I do feel we, as PWs, should go beyond paper plates and throwaway tableware. For many years it has been my policy, when having guests for more than one day, to plan a formal meal on the day of their arrival. I try to have my home as orderly as possible (whatever that is, and without apology). Because we are no longer pastoring and have mostly close friends and relatives visiting around our traveling schedules, I do things as easily as possible after that first formal meal. Breakfast is simple; the guests eat lunch whenever they are ready, often making their own sandwiches. The evening meal is the only one I plan.

I am a firm believer in serving food in an attractive way. Even if you are giving your guests nothing more than soup, salad, and bread, passing it to them in a silver bowl, or a beautiful glass one, can make them feel special. And don't reserve your best just for your guests! Whatever your best is, make sure your family also enjoys it at evening meals—if not every night, at least on special family occasions.

Hospitality is also a process of learning. I once taught a seminar to a group of Christian business women. Their week's assignment was to make one formal meal and serve it to their families. When the ladies returned to class for the next week's session, they were ecstatic. Those who had participated in the project were pleased about the attitudes of their husbands and children toward what they had done. One young woman admitted she had been so involved in church work, it had been a long time since she had taken needed time for her family. When her unsaved husband came home and found the lace tablecloth on the dining room table and a beautiful meal about to be served, he became much more responsive toward her. When their children came in the front door, after seeing the dining room table, they asked, "Hey, Mom, who's coming for dinner?" The mother, shocked by the response of her family, realized she had made them feel that her best was reserved for her guests.

Don't be afraid to try. You will never learn to be at ease while entertaining without first trying, making some mistakes, and doing other things well. All women have had their time of learning, being afraid, being cautious, not knowing just where or how to begin; but today's PW has every opportunity to develop herself in this area. "How-to" books are available on all aspects of informal and formal entertaining, such as the art of serving, table decor, and etiquette.

Hospitality Is Rewarding

Some of my most rewarding moments in life have been as I prepared and served dinner to the church board members and their wives. For many years it was an annual Christmas holiday affair, and then it became too much to handle during that hectic season. I also discovered that the group didn't care what time of year they came to the parsonage for a meal—they just enjoyed coming.

The secret to the success of the dinner was always in the planning and organization of the meal. I like to keep things elegantly simple, and for that reason a favorite for me was to prepare cornish game hens. They are not only easy to do, they are not time-consuming, are easily digested, and just about everyone can eat them. The remainder of my meal was planned around the meat dish, and was arranged as far ahead as possible.

Formal handwritten invitations were mailed no later than two weeks prior to the dinner, with the event being posted on the church calendar well in advance. Reservations were requested, and we encouraged our guests to wear their best dress clothes. Two to four teenagers were chosen and asked if they would like to serve the meal. One woman from our church made matching white tea aprons for the girls, who wore them with white blouses and dark skirts. Boys were encouraged to wear white shirts and black pants. Those serving were asked to come to the parsonage one hour early to get oriented and receive instructions on how the meal was to be served and in what order. The planned organizational procedure was also posted on the refrigerator so they would know exactly what was expected of them. This event became a highlight of the year as the youths felt especially honored to be involved in it. In most cases I would have one woman come to direct the kitchen while I remained with my guests.

This was also a learning time for all youths involved, as well as for others who might be assisting or eating with us. On one occasion, we were living in an area that was unconscious of social protocol. When my daughter Jan—home from college and with a strong feeling for the under-privileged—was told that we would be serving the formal board dinner she was terribly shocked. "Mother, don't you think these people will feel intimidated if you serve them with your silver, and have such a dinner?" When I explained to her my reasons, that those people deserved my very best—perhaps even more than those in other churches we had pastored—she understood. Surely enough, never have I served a group of people who ate more, enjoyed the evening as much, or were more appreciative than they. It was out of that time of eating together that many of the ladies in our church became challenged to rise above their methods of doing things in "just any old way" to one of taking pride in themselves and those things pertaining to the kingdom of God.

After all, isn't that what we are called to do as PWs—to draw out the best in everyone, to impart that which we have seen and heard in the lives of others, as we assume our roles as spiritual leaders in today's world? For this our labors will not go unrewarded.

> "And if, as my representatives, you give even a cup of cold water to a little child, you will surely be rewarded" (Matt. 10:42, TLB).

Suggested Reading:
Hall, Vivian Anderson, *Be My Guest,* Moody Press
Stewart, Martha, and Hawes, Elizabeth, *Entertaining,*
  Crown

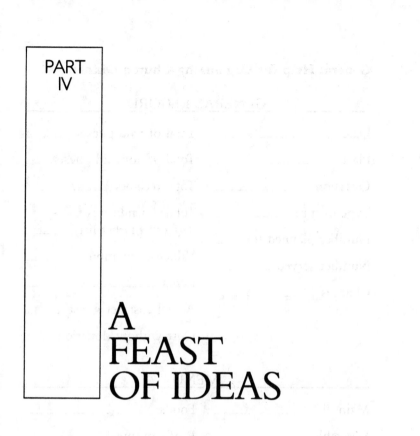

PART
IV

A
FEAST
OF IDEAS

General Help for Organizing Church Dinners

GENERAL RECORD

Date _____

Place _____

Occasion _____

Type of meal _____

Number planned for ___

Number served _____

Charges _____

Total of paid guests _____

Total of nonpaid guests ___

Total receipts _____

Total expenditures
  (from market list) _____

Value of donation _____

Items _____

Actual cost per guest _____

Cost without donations ___

MENU

Main dish _____

Vegetable _____

Relishes _____

Salad _____

Bread _____

Dessert _____

Drinks _____

Foods _____

Profit on meal _____

Paper service _____

Paper plates 9" _____

Paper plates 6" _____

Hot cups _____

Cold cups _____

EQUIPMENT CHAIRPERSON

If a chairperson is not available, arrange for help two days previous to the event for table setups. This allows the committee members to work on their individual setups that morning.

Price of hall _____

Place _____

Ticket chairperson _____

Prize chairperson _____

Membership _____

Hospitality chairperson _____

Hostess chairperson _____

GENERAL CHAIRPERSON

1. Personnel chairperson _____

2. Finance chairperson _____

3. Publicity chairperson _____

4. Equipment chairperson _____

5. Decorations chairperson _____

6. Hostess chairperson _____

7. Membership chairperson _____

8. Program chairperson _____

9. Other chairperson _____

Each chairperson is to give a report to the general chairperson.

MARKETING LIST

Number of Guests	Quantity to Buy	Cost	Donation (by whom & value)	Remarks
MEAT:				
FRUITS:				
DAIRY PRODUCTS:				
STAPLES NEEDED:				
DRINKS:				
PAPER SERVICE:				
Tablecloths				
Napkins				
Plates 9"				
Plates 6"				
Hot cups				
Cold cups				
TABLE DECORATIONS:				
Flowers				

FOOD BUYING GUIDE—FOR 100 PEOPLE

Item	Serving per person	100 Servings
Butter	2 tsp.	2¼ lbs.
Macaroni	1 cup cooked	11½ lbs.
Spaghetti	1 cup cooked	11 lbs.
Noodles	1 cup cooked	12½ lbs.

Item	Serving per person	100 Servings
Rice	1 cup cooked	12 lbs.
Cottage cheese	2 oz.	12½ lbs.
Whipped cream	1¼ tbsp.	1 qt.
Cantaloupe	½ cup cubed	34 lbs.
Strawberries	½ cup fresh	13 lbs.
(frozen)		29 lbs.
Green beans	½ cup	5 #10 cans
Beets (sliced)	½ cup	5 #10 cans
Cabbage (fresh		
shredded)		16 lbs.
Carrots	½ cup	5 #10 cans
(fresh cooked)		24 lbs.
Celery	one 2½" stick	4 bunches
Corn on cob	one	50 lbs.
(canned niblets)	½ cup	5 #10 cans
Potatoes, mashed	½ cup	31 lbs.
(baked)	one	37 lbs.
Sauerkraut	½ cup	5 #10 cans
Sweet potatoes	½ cup	34 lbs.
Tomatoes (sliced)		25 lbs.
Vegetables		
(mixed)	½ cup	21 lbs.
Juices	½ cup	8¾ (46 oz.) cans
Frozen concentrate	½ cup	17 (6 oz.) cans
3 to 1 (apple, grape,		3¼ (32 oz.) cans
grapefruit, orange)		

MEAT

Item	Serving per person	100 Servings
Beef (ground)	1 patty	17 lbs.
Roast (boneless)	4 oz.	38 lbs.
Roast chuck		
(bone in)	— —	44 lbs.
Round (bone in)	— —	42 lbs.
Stew meat (cooked)	2 oz.	18 lbs.

Item	Serving per person	100 Servings
Pork (cured, boneless)	4 oz.	40 lbs.
Ham	4 oz.	62 lbs.
Fresh pork	— —	68 lbs.
Roast loin	— —	62 lbs.
Sausage (link)	two	29 lbs.
Frankfurters	one	12½ lbs.
Luncheon meat	2 oz.	12½ lbs.
Chicken	2 pieces	42 lbs.
(stewed)	— —	40 lbs.
(canned, boneless, salad)	— —	12½ lbs.
Turkey	3 oz.	51 lbs.
Salmon	2 oz.	16 (16 oz.) cans
Tuna	2 oz.	24 (7 oz.) cans
Dried salt cod	2 oz.	17½ lbs.
Fillets	4 oz.	40 lbs.
Oysters	2 oz.	4 gal.
Shrimp (fresh)	2 oz.	12½ lbs.
Jams & jellies	2 tbsp.	6 lbs.
Nuts	— —	6 lbs.
(Mixed for nut cups)	— —	3 lbs.
Olives	3 or 4	4 qts.
Peanut butter	4 tbsp.	14½ lbs.
Salad dressing	1 tbsp.	1¾ qts.
French	1⅓ tbsp.	2½ qts.
Syrup	2 tbsp.	¾ gal.

BEVERAGES

	Serving per person	100 Servings
Cocoa, coffee	6 cups	5 gal.
Tea, hot & cold	8 oz.	6 gal.

BREADS

	Serving per person	100 Servings
Bread	2 slices	14 loaves
Brown, nut orange	— —	10 loaves
Rolls	one	8½ doz.

Item	Serving per person	100 Servings
Rolls, raised	Men–3 oz.	Men–18 doz.
	Women–1½ oz.	Women–12 doz.
Cornbread	2 oz. (or 2 muffins)	18 doz.
Muffins	— —	18 doz.
Griddle cakes	two	13 qts. batter
Doughnuts	two	18 doz.
Toast & butter	2 slices	14 lbs.
Layer cakes, 3 (10″ layers)	2½ oz.	6 cakes
Cupcakes	one	100 cupcakes
Angel cakes	1 oz.	6 (10″ cakes)
Ice cream	½ cup	16 qts. (#12 dip)
Pie (8″)	one (6-7 cuts)	16 pies

CAN SIZES

7 #300 is approximately 1 #10 can
6 #303 is approximately 1 #10 can
5 #2 is approximately 1 #10 can
4 #2½ is approximately 1 #10 can
3 46 oz. is approximately 1 #10 can

MEASUREMENT TABLE

Some recipes call for ingredients measured by the spoonful while others call for them in ounces. Here is a handy table to clip and file to compare measurements.

1 cube butter equals	½ cup
4 tbsp. equal	¼ cup
3 tsp. equal	1 tbsp.
½ oz. fluid equals	1 tbsp.
16 tbsp. equal	1 cup
8 oz. fluid equals	1 cup
1 pt. equals	2 cups

2 pts. equal	*1 qt.*
4 cups equal	*1 qt.*
60 drops equal	*1 tbsp.*
16 oz. equal	*1 lb.*
8 cups equal	*1 gal.*
4 qts. equal	*1 gal.*
1 cup equals	*8 oz.*
¾ cup milk equals	*¼ cup dry milk plus 1 cup water*
1 cup butter equals	*½ lb.*
1 cup lard equals	*½ lb.*
1 oz. chocolate equals	*1 square*
1 lb. cocoa equals	*4 cups*
1 lb. flour (all purpose) equals	*4 cups sifted*
1 lb. brown sugar equals	*2¼ cups packed*
1 lb. granulated sugar equals	*2 cups*
1 lb. confectioners sugar equals	*3½ cups sifted*
½ lb. rice equals	*1 cup*
¼ lb. cornstarch equals	*1 cup*
1 lb. cornmeal equals	*3 cups*

Since bread is a major cost item to consider in preparing for a large group, these recipes may be helpful to you.

Ruthe's Basic Biscuit Mix (serves 20-30 people)
10 cups flour
16 tsp. or half cup (heaped) baking powder
5 tsp. salt
2 cups shortening
½ cup margarine
2 tsp. cream of tartar

Sift all dry ingredients together. Work shortening through with hands until it is mealy. Place in refrigerator overnight.

Just before baking, use one quart of buttermilk to mix. If dough is a little stiff, add a little more liquid. Roll out and cut. Bake at 425°, approximately 20 minutes.

Dry ingredients can be made up and stored in deep freeze or refrigerator. If smaller amounts of mixture are to be used, add just enough milk for a stiff dough.

LARGE QUANTITY CORNBREAD

Cornbread Mix
100 Portions

Weights	Measures	Ingredients
3 lbs.	3 qt., sifted	All-purpose flour
4½ oz.	¾ cup	Baking powder
10 oz.	1¼ cups	Sugar
1½ oz.	3 tbsp.	Salt
2 lb. 8 oz.	2 qt.	Cornmeal
10 oz.	2½ cups	Nonfat dry milk

Directions:
1. Sift ingredients together three times or blend 15 minutes in mixer on low speed, using the whisk.
2. Store in a tightly covered container in a cool place until needed.

Yield: 7 lbs. (1¼ gallons, 1½ cups)

Cornbread (using cornbread mix)

7 lbs.	1¼ gal. 1½ cups	Cornbread mix
	2 cups (10)	Eggs
	2½ qt.	Water
1 lb. 4 oz.	2½ cups	Melted shortening

Directions:
3. Combine cornbread mix with remaining ingredients and mix just enough to moisten.
4. Pour into four well-greased baking pans (12"x18"x2").
5. Bake at 415°F. (hot) 30 to 40 minutes.

Portion: 1 piece (2"x3")

VARIATION

Cornmeal Muffins: Portion batter with a #16 scoop (¼ cup) into greased muffin pans. Bake at 425° (hot) 20 minutes.

MUFFINS

Muffin Mix
100 Portions

Weights	Measures	Ingredients
4 lbs.	1 gal., sifted	All-purpose flour
8 oz.	2 cups	Nonfat dry milk
4 oz.	⅔ cup	Baking powder
1¼ oz.	2½ tbsp.	Salt
10 oz.	1¼ cup	Sugar

Directions:
1. Sift ingredients together three times or blend 15 minutes in mixer on low speed, using the whisk.
2. Store in a tightly covered container in a cool place until needed.

Yield: 5 lbs. 8 oz. (4½ qt.)

Plain Muffins (using muffin mix)

12 oz.	1½ cups	Melted shortening
	1½ cups (8)	Eggs, beaten
	1¼ qt.	Water
5 lb. 8 oz.	4½ qt., sifted	Muffin mix

Directions:
3. Combine shortening with eggs, then add the water.
4. Add to muffin mix. Stir only until dry ingredients are moist and the mixture has a rough appearance.
5. Using a #24 scoop (2⅔ tbsp.), portion into greased muffin pans.
6. Bake at 425°F. (hot) 15 minutes.

Portion: 1 muffin

VARIATIONS

Blueberry Muffins: Add 2 cups raw or drained canned blueberries to the shortening mixture.

Date Muffins: Add 1 lb. (2⅓ cups) chopped dates to the muffin mix.

Raisin Muffins: Add 10 oz. (2 cups) raisins to the muffin mix.

TWO EASY SIDE DISHES
AND MY MOST REQUESTED RECIPES

Pineapple/Banana/Peanut Salad

1 small can Spanish salted peanuts
1 4 oz. can drained cubed pineapple
8 large firm bananas
1 cup sugar
1 egg
3 tbsp. vinegar or lemon juice (I prefer lemon juice)
1 tbsp. Tang (optional)
3 tbsp. water

Put sugar, lemon juice, water, Tang, and egg into a small saucepan. Whisk the ingredients together until frothy and place on medium heat. Continue whipping and stirring until the sauce begins to boil. Boil two minutes longer, stirring continuously. Remove from heat and place in a covered glass container and chill. When sauce is cold it will be the consistency of a thick syrup.

Just before serving, slice the bananas into 1/8" rounds, toss with the well-drained pineapple and crushed peanuts. You can garnish with toasted coconut, cherries, and a few whole peanuts. This makes an excellent side dish with meat and is quite filling.

Pizza Bread Supreme (Teenagers and men love this!)
2 lbs. extra lean ground beef
1 cube margarine
1 pkg. dry spaghetti seasoning
1 lb. Velveeta cheese
1 bell pepper
1 medium onion
1 can tomato sauce
2 cans chopped or sliced black olives
Parmesan cheese
Green pimiento olives for garnish

Sauté finely chopped onions and bell peppers in a small amount of margarine until the onions are clear in color. Remove to a large mixing bowl. Cook hamburger that is broken into small pieces (use potato masher to break it up while cooking). Stir meat but do not brown. When it is cooked through, dump into mixing bowl with onions and peppers, add cheese, butter, tomato sauce, seasonings, and black olives. Stir until cheese and butter are melted. Store in covered container or freeze in small portions. (Better if allowed to sit twenty-four hours.)

When serving, spread over sliced French rolls, sour dough, or rye bread. Lay bread on greased cookie sheet, spread each slice with the mixture (lay one on top of other, three deep, but stagger them as you stack them), top each slice with a green pimiento olive, sprinkle with parmesan cheese, bake at 425° 15 minutes or until slightly brown on top. When serving a crowd, just keep browning and serving one layer at a time.
(Serves 20)

PASTORS' WIVES QUESTIONNAIRE
(Women in Partnership Ministry)

NAME: _____

ADDRESS: _____

CITY: _____

STATE: _____

DENOMINATION: _____

APPROXIMATE SIZE OF CONGREGATION: _____

DO YOU HAVE CHILDREN? _____

  CHILDREN'S AGES: (1-5) (6-10) (11-18)

Personal Data: (Leave out any answers you do not wish to give)

1. What do you enjoy most about you/your husband's ministry?

   _____

2. What do you least enjoy about your work/ministry? _____

   _____

3. What is the most difficult area in which you have had to learn to cope?

   _____ Why? _____

4. Do you feel fulfilled, as a woman, in your role as a pastor's wife? ____

5. Do you see your role as: (a) being a wife to your husband but not involved in the church work itself (b) moderately involved (c) mainly a low-profile person (d) highly visible and active (e) confused about your role and what is expected of you?

6. If you could change one thing about your role as a pastor's wife what

   would it be? _____Why? _____

7. Did you have a pastor's wife who provided you with a positive/negative role model as: (a) child (b) teenager (c) later in life (d) not at all?

8. Tell how and why _____

9. Do you find yourself resenting your role: (a) occasionally (b) never

   (c) almost always? If your answer was (c), tell why _____

   _____

10. Do you consider yourself as being active in church ministry? _____

11. Do you work on a secular job? _____ How many hours weekly? _____

Church Related:

12. Do you live in a church-owned parsonage/manse? _____ How long? _____

13. Do you live in your own home? _____ rent? _____

14. Have you ever owned equity in your own home? _____

15. Does living in the parsonage make you feel: (a) secure (b) insecure (c) a source of problem (d) no problem at all?
16. Do you feel accepted by most of the parishioners: (a) usually (b) all the time (c) sometimes (d) hardly at all?
17. Do you feel you are accepted by the church on the basis of who you are as a person rather than who your husband is? _____
18. Do you presently feel overworked with responsibilities of church duties: (a) somewhat (b) not at all (c) very much so (d) tired of it all?
19. Do you feel called to any one particular area of church ministry? ____
20. Are you presently working in the area of what you consider "your calling"? _____
21. Does your church consider you as part of its staff? _____
22. In what areas of the church do you presently work? _____
23. Do you feel: (a) secure (b) happy (c) unhappy about your work?
24. Would you like to be: (a) more active in the church (b) less active?
25. Tell why _____

Husband:
26. Does your husband recognize your personal needs: (a) almost always (b) seldom (c) doesn't have time or take time to hear you (d) very understanding of your needs?
27. Would your husband like you to: (a) be more active in church work (b) be less active (c) just be there when he needs you (d) be your own woman?
28. Was your husband in the ministry/seminary/training when you married him? _____
29. Do you feel the church demands too much of both him and you? ____
30. Do you socialize with women inside the church: (a) exclusively (b) some (c) just a few close friends among them (d) only church-related social functions?

General:
31. If you had a personal need or problem would you go to: (a) your husband (b) another minister's wife (c) another minister in the same group with which you and your husband are associated (d) someone outside of your particular church organization?
32. If you have children, do you feel they are: (a) resentful of being pastor's kids (b) understanding of your work and accept it reasonably well (c) totally accepting of themselves and others and unaffected by your work?

33. If you could begin in the ministry again, what is the one thing you would do differently in your work? _____
34. What is the one thing you would like to tell every young minister's wife?

_____

35. Why is the above so important to you? _____
36. How many years have you and your husband been in church-related ministry? _____

Do you have something you would like to say? Write me:

RUTHE WHITE
P. O. Box 1346
Crestline, CA 92325